The Urbana Free Library

To renew: call 217-367-4057
or go to "*urbanafreelibrary.org*"
and select "Renew/Request Items"

+2-12

$$f P$$

THE BOOKS
THEY GAVE ME

True Stories of Life, Love, and Lit

JEN ADAMS

FREE PRESS

New York   London   Toronto   Sydney   New Delhi

12/12
1999

FREE PRESS
A Division of Simon & Schuster, Inc.
1230 Avenue of the Americas
New York, NY 10020

First Free Press hardcover edition November 2012

FREE PRESS and colophon are trademarks of Simon & Schuster, Inc.

For information about special discounts for bulk purchases,
please contact Simon & Schuster Special Sales at 1-866-506-1949
or business@simonandschuster.com.

The Simon & Schuster Speakers Bureau can bring authors to your live event.
For more information or to book an event contact the Simon & Schuster Speakers Bureau at 1-866-248-3049 or visit our website at www.simonspeakers.com.

DESIGNED BY ERICH HOBBING

Manufactured in the United States of America

1   3   5   7   9   10   8   6   4   2

Library of Congress Cataloging-in-Publication Data
The books they gave me /[compiled by] Jen Adams.
pages cm
Selected contributions from the blog, TheBooksTheyGaveMe.com, edited by Jen Adams.
1. Books and reading—Psychological aspects. 2. Books and reading—
Miscellanea. 3. Gifts—Miscellanea. 4. Interpersonal relations—Miscellanea.
I. Adams, Jen, 1974—. II. Title.
Z1003.B725 2012
028'9—dc23   2012017262

ISBN 978-1-4516-8879-5
ISBN 978-1-4516-8881-8 (ebook)

for John and Edward

CONTENTS

Contents

Contents

Contents

Contents

Contents

Contents

INTRODUCTION

J. Alfred Prufrock measured his life out in coffee spoons. I measure mine out in pages. I am the archetypal bookworm, never without a book in my bag and four more in progress on my nightstand. My apartment is filled with books. In fact, when I was looking for a place here in New York, my primary requirement was that the apartment offered enough wall space to house all my bookcases. In short, books are my language, my vocabulary. Every experience in my life is filtered through what I've read and somehow processed in prose. I'm constantly reading and constantly writing. And anyone who knows me well must understand and accept this about me. The books are nonnegotiable. They are part of me. They *are* me.

So, when a man I was dating brought me an especially well-chosen book as a gift, I realized in a flash that, for those of us who live for the written word, books given and received in the context of a relationship can reveal so much. This observation is well documented in popular culture. In Woody Allen's film *Annie Hall,* Annie and Alvy sort out their respective books as they are breaking up. Annie realizes that the relationship may have always been doomed—Alvy only ever gave her books with "death" in the title.

In one episode of the late 1980s TV series *The Days and Nights of Molly Dodd,* Molly's ex-husband surprises her at work (in a bookshop, natch) one blustery cold night. Defensively, he says, "You know, I gave Molly some books once. Remember? Twenty-seventh birthday? Twenty-seven books." Her current lover, bookshop owner Moss, appreciates this. "Books make nice gifts." But

Molly remembers well: "You gave me twenty-seven *comic* books, Frank. Not *real* books." Frank failed the test, without even knowing he was taking one.

Sometimes, we put suitors to the test with full knowledge of what we are doing. In Martin Amis's novel *Money,* Martina Twain gives the supplicant John Self a copy of *Animal Farm,* telling him that he needs to read it. He tries and fails, and never gets very far with Martina.

Books can also have potent influences over us; giving someone the right book at the right time can change his life forever—to wit, the little yellow-covered book Lord Henry Wotton gives to Dorian in Oscar Wilde's *The Picture of Dorian Gray.* The suggestions of sensual excess in the book set Dorian off on a path that leads to corruption and utter ruin. More often, we hear of books that change lives for the better. In Louisa May Alcott's *Little Women,* Beth, Jo, and their sisters are each given a copy of *The Pilgrim's Progress* as their only Christmas gift in a straitened, wartime year. The book becomes a spiritual guidebook as well as an imaginative one that will illuminate and shape their lives. And the effect of books on real people's lives can be as powerful, as the stories in *The Books They Gave Me* will reveal.

At home, as I shelved my boyfriend's gift book, I touched the spines of other books I'd been given by men I'd loved. The beautiful hardcover edition of the complete poems of William Blake. A picture book, a tongue-in-cheek response to the rise of the e-book. A slim little paperback reprint of lyric poetry. Each of them, I realized, said something important about who we were at that moment. The books I own tell my life story, and the ones given me by the people I love offer special insight into the experiences that have made me who I am.

I began to collect stories of gifted books, and decided to compile them in that most modern of diaristic forms, the blog. Stories began to pour in to TheBooksTheyGaveMe.com from all over the world as word spread and other readers decided to share their experiences. Some are wryly funny; some will make you cry or ball your fists in anger. I began saving the best of them, having realized that a book compiling these stories is one that I'd love to read and own.

I've been moved profoundly by my readers' submissions. They've told me of their loves, those they lost and those they're lucky enough to be with. Their books are an important part of their identities and their personal histories. There's something magical about this blog and the reaction to it—it is causing people to look at their shelves—and at the habit of owning, sharing, and giving books—with new eyes.

In this age of the e-book, part of the appeal of being given a hard copy book as a gift is its tangible timelessness. Books are real. You can give a book as a gift. Kindles are great for reading on the subway, and they get people to read more than they might otherwise, but they are flatly unromantic. Paper books offer a kind of permanent charm. They don't expire; they can't disappear in a power surge. Books last. I'm not with any of those men anymore, but I still have the books they gave me.

BURROUGHS
Dry

This book was lent to me by one of the most important people in my life.

She was my girlfriend at the time and I loved her unconditionally, despite my skepticism of love and our young age. One day she handed me this book, and as I read the words that were etched into the rough-edged paper, I knew I was in love. I bought the book myself shortly after, reading and rereading the pages over and over until the lines began to blur and the pages wore thin. And even though she never actually bought and gave me the book, she gave me the contents of the book.

She gave me the words that stilled my mind and opened my heart. It's nothing more than a memoir, but it's something I'll never forget.

PERNICE
Meat Is Murder

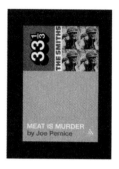

He, professor of the way things are going to be, the way we are going to be entertained in the future, knew I love The Smiths. Despite growing up in England in the eighties, he doesn't like them at all. He loves American music, rap and funk and hip-hop. We met after work one day at some trendy hole in the wall café on the UES that serves nothing but craft beers and grilled-cheese sandwiches. (This is not a criticism; that was the best damn grilled cheese I have ever eaten.) He pulled from his back pocket a slim little novella. It was from the 33⅓ series published by Continuum—Joe Pernice's *Meat Is Murder*.

I felt, rightly or wrongly, that this meant he understood how powerful and precious our connections to the music we love can be. Though he disagreed powerfully with my musical loves ("poncey limey whingers," he called them all) and I was indifferent to the charms of his, he never challenged them or pressed me to defend them. This book meant that he understood.

YEATS
The Collected Poems of W. B. Yeats

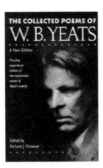

I told her I liked Yeats, and a week later she gave me a copy of his *Collected Poems.* I thought this was odd, as of course I had a copy; he was my favorite poet. So I hid my copy.

When we moved in together, she found my hidden copy. "Why didn't you tell me you had it?" she asked.

"Because I was so happy that you thought of me, this is the only copy I wanted to read."

We were married before the end of the year.

COELHO
By the River Piedra I Sat Down and Wept

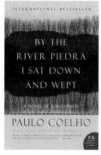

A few years ago I read Paulo Coelho's *By the River Piedra I Sat Down and Wept*. I convinced my then-boyfriend to read it because I myself was convinced that the story bore a ghostly resemblance to our own love story—a story that, unbeknownst to either of us at the time, was approaching a grave ending. I made notes in the margins, highlighting passages I knew he would love because they were beautifully wrought, and those I knew he would contemplate because they touched upon the spiritual and echoed his own quest for a spiritual awakening. He did, in fact, love them.

Tonight, in need of inspiration, I had the urge to pick up the book and read through my notes.

I couldn't find the book.

And then I remembered that he'd never returned my copy. And, like a flash, a post-breakup conversation resurfaced in my memory. He had told me that after our breakup he'd carried the book with him and reread the story and all of my scribbles as an attempt to cling onto some piece of me when we were no longer speaking.

As I sat on my knees, surrounded by piles of books, remembering all of this, it occurred to me that sharing books is an intimate act in a relationship. If sharing music is considered an act of foreplay—which it is to me anyway—then sharing books is definitely going all the way. With music, you merely glimpse your infatuation's tastes. Still, it's easy to tune out a song you don't particularly care for when you would rather listen to him talk or relish the comfort of his arms. But with books, you pay attention. You're reading words; you're consuming ideas and themes that move him; you're connecting intellectually. Maybe even spiritually.

I could be overthinking this. But I can't help but feel a sense of loss knowing that my book, marked by my handwriting—the ideas and phrases that spoke to me now exposed, underlined, circled, highlighted—is floating in the world.

Just like a man I once loved.

MULFORD
Love Poems by Women

We argued over poetry. I made the (foolish, pigheaded) case that there are no great female poets. She gave me this book and announced that we were going out. It lasted two weeks and then, just as abruptly as it had started, she announced that we were done. I no longer believe there are no great female poets, but this book had nothing to do with my change.

ROMBAUER
The Joy of Cooking

At first, I bristled. I mean, what kind of guy gives his boyfriend a cookbook? It's not like I'm known for cooking. I can't cook. What was he trying to say, "I'd love you more if you were more domestic"?

But then he opened the book. "Look, see? Look at these . . ." he flipped through pages filled with recipes for canapés and dips and fancy spreads. "We could have cocktail parties. We could make this stuff; there's nothing hard about it. We could do it together, and have our friends come over." He slipped an arm around my waist. My indignation dissolved. He wasn't trying to dominate me or make me fit some weird mold. His little dream of sophisticated cocktail parties (in our studio? really?) was a dream of the life we could build together. We would entertain, we would be a couple; we would be the center of a warm group of friends. It was a beautiful dream.

NOBODY

I have never received a book from anyone. From a friend, a lover, a parent, or anyone. I've gotten gift cards to Borders, Barnes & Noble, local stores, and cash meant for books. But I have never actually gotten a physical book from anyone. I actually like it better that way. I think that letting me make the choice about the book I want is better. I would like to get a book from someone who knows me and knows exactly what I want, but I have yet to encounter that person. I believe that giving a book to a person is like giving a piece of your soul to them. You have to open yourself up to giving the person a piece of yourself, a part of your mind, and a little bit of your body. It's a personal gift, a book, and it's something that shouldn't be taken lightly. So when you give a book, make sure you're prepared to be as open as you've ever been.

BEATTY & DIXON & LOPEZ & MARTIN
Batgirl: Year One

We met online. He wasn't my first boyfriend, but he was the first person I truly fell in love with. Some of our very first dates were spent in used bookstores. We are both literature nerds, and he also shared with me his love of comic books and graphic novels. He introduced me to Batgirl, now one of my favorite superheroines because Barbara Gordon is a librarian and I want to become a librarian.

Our relationship isn't perfect. Each of us is in a state of transition in our lives and neither of us has any idea where we will be a year from now. We have our differences and our rough patches. I have no idea if he's "the one" or if the future will see us still together.

I do know that he has had a tremendous amount of faith in and hope for our relationship, and that alone is the nicest present anyone could have ever given me. This comic book, his Christmas present to me, is a close second.

HARVEY
The Chicago Way

I froze when she gave me this. I feared she had guessed, or heard something. What she didn't know, I couldn't tell her. I had secrets in Chicago, and I knew that if she knew about them, she wouldn't love me anymore. And I was right. I finally told her, and she never looked at me the same way again. It was over by the time the truth was out of my mouth.

ANONYMOUS

It was all I could keep of him. Our affair started shortly after his marriage began and ended shortly before the birth of his child. One night, after walking through a local park, we sat and watched the stars.

Telling each other stories in between stolen kisses, I only wished I could have loved him sooner. The next morning there was a bag in my car with this book and a note. These were his stories, poems, and drawings. I held on to that book for five years. One day, when cleaning out old boxes, my current boyfriend found the book. When he saw what power those words still had, he convinced me to get rid of it. Months later my former lover would walk into my life, only to be torn away again. Part of me wishes I could have held on to them, to those words, and to him. I am grateful for the man who realized how harmful those words were. For the man who had the power to set me free.

TALEB
The Black Swan:
The Impact of the Highly Improbable

Being a reader of fiction, when I needed a nonfiction book, he was the one I turned to. He gave me this, one of his recent favourites, I took it for the title.

I was blown away, and was only at the prologue. It's about the impact of the highly improbable. I'd like to think that explains our relationship.

Reading this book, knowing it was one of his favourites, made me enjoy it that much more.

I feel as if I know him on a level that no one else does, because we've shared a mutual love for a book.

He is not my boyfriend of six years, but I feel like I know him better than I do my boyfriend.

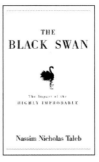

I wish my boyfriend would give me books and share my love for books and reading.

I currently have not finished the book because I don't want to lose the connection that it brings—or explain the connection we have.

BURROUGHS
Possible Side Effects

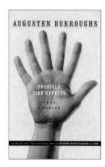

We had always been day-late lovers, meeting under the right circumstances but at the wrong times. Much older than I, she had wisdom, pain, and above all, a love for music and literature that could not be surpassed.

One evening, spent mostly naked in her bed, she reached behind her nightstand and revealed a book. I can remember observing that it was so yellow, in comparison to her porcelain skin.

"I want you to have this, to keep you distracted from things you needn't be involved with, when I am not around," she whispered, with a halfhearted smirk. She inscribed her name, and the words "With love" upon the index page, a permanent reminder of herself.

"Read to me," she whispered. "I find comfort in your voice; you read like my mother did. I cannot help but observe the contours of your face as you speak." Her mother had died, and I felt as though I could almost reach, pull apart the sadness in her eyes as these words rolled from her tongue.

We spent a long night laughing, her head in my lap. I read until my throat was raw, until the feeling of her lips on my jawline had become a distraction I couldn't bear any longer. It became a ritual on nights where we would give in to our lust; she would reach behind to reveal the memoir, and I would read to her until our bodies couldn't fight it anymore.

Three months after we broke up, with my own copy of the book, I hadn't even so much as touched the cover. The book brought constant reminders of the aftermath of a forgotten love. She had taken flight from my life, finding resignation in her sadness, but leaving me with these hardcover words.

And on days where the weight of the world seems unbearable, I pick up the book and hold it, momentarily, hoping to find the pieces of her I found those nights. The book she gave me is the only method I have: a method of finding resignation in my own sadness, and remembering that at some point, our love was real.

The Life and Doctrine of St. Catherine of Genoa

My best friend from Oxford called his antiques dealer in Geneva, described me in great detail, and said, "Find her something perfect." It was my birthday. He sent a mottled, leather-covered, gilt-embossed *Life and Doctrine of St. Catherine of Genoa*. On the frontispiece, the willowy saint bent her golden head over a tall lily she held in one hand. The spine was soft, loose, starting to disintegrate. The book was hundreds of years old. It was entirely in French.

When he gave it to me, I told him I wouldn't be able to read it. How could I keep a secret while holding the life of a saint in my hands? It must have sounded like ingratitude, and he, who had taken me to meet the queen, who had invited me to dinner at Christ Church high table and cocktails at the East India Club, would certainly register that familiar, slight, unconcealable dismay that I didn't know the only language civilized people spoke. In the past, when I had admitted I didn't know French, people had said, "That changes my entire image of you," or "Could we pretend you didn't just say that?" "It's all right," he said without blinking, "It's important to have books in languages one doesn't read."

I found a small mahogany table whose round top wasn't much larger than the book itself, and put it beneath a faint Fragonard sketch of the Madonna and child, made in Rome, on his Grand Tour, before he was twenty. It was his first time away from home. He was copying Andrea del Sarto, known as a master *senza errori,* without error. But the Fragonard sketch looks nothing like the original. His unfaithful Madonna, with her rosebud pout, and the baby, wild, clinging to her, looking away.

One part of that room is arranged around the book now: the Fragonard in its gold-painted wooden frame with tiny, intertwined flowers; the unlit candle in thick jade glass near the book, scented to evoke a Carmelite cloister: iris and spices, sandalwood and cedar.

Years later the man who gave me the book said he didn't speak French either. He told me casually, after a long dinner in New York. Oxford seemed so far away then, and we had settled in at home. He wore cuff links given to his father by a president. They had flags, or eagles, on them. We were back to being Americans.

"We must not wish anything other than what happens," wrote Saint Catherine, "from moment to moment."

DE SAINT-EXUPÉRY
Le Petit Prince

Once my dad's high school French teacher—and later, his close friend—talked my parents into putting me into French immersion classes. I was a quick learner. My days were happily bilingual, vacillating between *en Français s'il-te-plait* and "again, in English please." You gave me your battered copy of *Le Petit Prince,* and together we read it over and over again until the pages curled up; the salt of my fingers heaved at the spine of the thin book until it was hunchbacked and threadbare—we used the dark ribbons of its text to tie the two languages of our thoughts snugly together. Despite the gap of decades between us, we became fast friends.

On our many ski trips you spent hours with me while my family members were out expertly navigating the slopes. At the time, my young uncoordinated body had been exiled to the T-bars, but the slow drag up the hill was icy and underwhelming and I'd tired of it quickly. I was forbidden to bench myself with my older siblings on the dangling chairlifts that scaled the side of the precipitous mountain. I played at pouting, but I took care not to protest too much—the slow heavy clanking of the chairs on the thin cord seemed menacing from the reassuring safety of the mountain's base. Instead, pencil crayons in hand, we drew together at the chalet's kitchen table most afternoons while you encouraged me to work on my conversational French; I painstakingly illustrated dozens of images of you, choosing to depict your moustached face on a wobbly version of the Fox from chapter 11.

"*Renard?*" I asked. In French, you were always the Fox.

"*Oui, Mademoiselle?*" you said, but when I glowered you corrected yourself: "*Oh! Je suis désolé. Pardonnez-moi—oui, mon Petit Prince?*"

"*Pourquoi personne ne veut que le Petit Prince leur poser des questions?*" I couldn't understand why the grown-ups in the book didn't like it when le Petit Prince asked questions—why it made them angry, uncomfortable, or sad.

"*Parce que les gens n'aiment pas la réalization qu'ils ont aucun meilleure réponse à lui offrir.*" He sighed and pulled on his moustache before looking at me sharply out of the corner of his eye. "*Poser des questions, mon Petit Prince. N'ayez pas peur.* Do you hear me—ask questions, be brave, never fear curiosity, *mon p'tit chou*, okay? Don't be afraid."

The week before you returned to Québec you assured me that you would join my family out west the following month for spring break. Skiing was a March tradition for us; it would have been a solitary and monotonous week for me on the T-bars without you. Just before you squeezed yourself into your eastbound two-door sedan, carefully packed with all your worldly possessions, you slipped me a small box, plainly wrapped. Inside were mittens that had tiny foxes knitted into them—their pinched faces were burnt orange and inscrutable.

A dozen years passed and by the time I was in university we hardly spoke except a few moments each December on Christmas Day. I hadn't had anyone else to practice my French with and the verbal dexterity of our infrequent conversations became less fluent with disuse, less intimate. By the time I was twenty-two I realized that, though I could still understand Radio-Canada *en Français* I had forfeited the ability to speak the language—the conjugations had become unfamiliar.

It was raining one evening when my father called to tell me you had died. I reeled, my spine heaved as I unravelled at the loss of you. That summer a family of foxes moved into the space under my parents' boathouse. Near the water, cold amber eyes and vermilion tails skulked uninvitingly nearby and at dusk I could hear low growls, menacing and getting closer each day. I started avoiding the area altogether, opting to read closer to the house in a hammock that my father had looped between two sturdy birch trees. From the safe distance of the latticed sling I spent the summer watching the kits as they revelled in the bloody fur of their spoils; on the chipstone path I'd find bones everywhere.

Over the years I'd shared English versions of *Le Petit Prince* for graduations or birthdays, but some subtleties had been lost in the translation.

"How is this a children's book?" one friend asked me. Her six-year-old was running around us in her kitchen. "You do know the Little Prince dies at the end, right? It's far too scary for a child."

Skiing in Jasper that last time, you held my ski poles for me and tugged up my scarf and pulled me onto the chairlift's seat and up into the wet, cold sky. As we settled in, I puffed out my cheeks and blew spit bubbles that burst instantly in the chilly air while you reclined cheerfully, glorying in the setting sun as you crowed—*"la colour du blé!*" Perhaps we should have felt guilty for disregarding my parents' orders, but the untamed beauty of the Alberta skyline made the occasion far too thrilling for contrition.

We had barely begun our ascent when Dad happened to ski past below the chairline and spotted us. He shook his ski poles up at us wildly as we sat thirty feet above his head on our unsteady perch. His rebuke rang in the air, resonating in the mountain's reverberating bowl. You hooted and waved cheekily back at him, I clapped my muffled hands over my mouth in delight and horror—you took one look at the eyes popping out of my dismayed face and burst into laughter before you threw back your head and swore you were dead in love with me—pulling my hood down over my eyes and tweaking my thick braid playfully. I grinned, righted my cap, and put my small mittened hand in the crook of your arm and we soon fell into easy silence. The punishment for our escapade would be forthcoming, but there was nothing to do at the moment except enjoy the ride while it lasted. We looked at each other, giddy with misbehaviour, and a profound gratefulness hummed through my chattering teeth and rooted itself in my bones. The chair creaked and I closed my eyes against the cool flakes that drifted onto my face. The lift ride was over far too soon. You raised the safety bar at the end of the line and cued me on how to alight the ramp gracefully. At the last moment the wind picked up unexpectedly and the chair pulled us forward into an eddy of snow. You lifted your ski tips and turned to face me, eyelashes white with snowflakes, and I heard your warm, familiar French accent teasing me: "*Tu encore peur, mon Prince?*" Eyes steadfastly towards the dismount, I smiled and shook my head no; the snow held us up like a hundred thousand hands—there was nothing to be afraid of.

GREGORY
Unpossible and Other Stories

My father loved science fiction and fantasy novels. Over the years he kept passing on full-length novels of the genre, hoping that it might ignite something we could have in common. I would get through a chapter or two and push the books away, not finding them interesting in the least, constantly disappointing my father.

Right before he died last year he gave me a copy of *Unpossible* by Daryl Gregory. Having just gotten a promotion at work, I was too busy at work to read it when he initially gave it to me. In the wake of his unexpected passing and in an attempt to assuage my grief I picked the book up, trying to find some connection with him I may have regretfully missed during his living years.

I ended up enjoying this book more than any of the others—maybe because they were short stories and not a full-length novel—more than I ever thought I could. The  book was entertainment beyond measure, but it also helped me get through. It has encouraged me to read more science fiction, not only because of my newfound love of the genre, but also as a way to remember my father—for the diehard sci-fi nerd and the great man that he was.

PERCY
The Moviegoer

The first guy I dated after I moved from Alabama to New York was a nerdy, adorable librarian. Six months after things had fizzled between us, I ran into him on the Lower East Side.

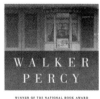

"It's funny running into you like this," he said, "I just read a book that reminded me a lot of you."

"Oh really?" I asked, my ego already blossoming into full bloom.

"Well . . . one of the more minor characters reminded me of you. I thought about calling you, but it didn't seem right."

"You're not going to tell me the name of the book?" I teased.

He had the book on him, took it out of his backpack and handed it to me.

"You can have it," he said nonchalantly, a big gesture in itself. As a librarian he carefully guarded all his books, never loaning them out. "I think you'll really enjoy it."

I did enjoy the book, but I quickly learned that it was not the wistful, beautifully complicated heroine that reminded him of me. Rather, it was the male protagonist's sassy secretary (also from Alabama), who was sexy but alarmingly simpleminded.

My ego is now back down to its normal level.

MILTON
Complete Poetry and Essential Prose

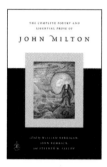

Words are beautiful; strung together in the right sequence, they can tell us the most magnificent stories, take us to the most beautiful places, and carry our hearts to the greatest heights.

My first love failed to feel this; my first love failed to last, lapsed at a lack of meeting intellect.

My second love, my new love, my all-encompassing, requited love, he spoke up for me once long before I knew him the way I know him now. At the cancer treatment and research institute where we both committed our time and emotions, another declared that, at first glance, my unassertive beauty, wispy bangs, and black-rimmed glasses called out "book nerd," and before I could meekly question, "What's the harm in that?" S stole my words. He read constantly, he said, consumed literature, piece after piece. He was an English major, attractive, intelligent, confident, and adventurous. I found him a little exceptional.

I still do. S was the first boy to give me a book, the first boy to read my books. Upon a few impressive shares, we vowed to read each other's favorites. He got lost in *East of Eden* and gave me his bulky, old-fashioned hardcover collection of the works of John Milton. *Paradise Lost* is his favorite work, but I was lost in it all, the sonnets, the masterpieces, the prose. I was lost in the conversations we could share, the way he could speak to my soul through words so beautiful. I was lost in the love I had found.

We met in Michigan, but neither of us is there any longer. S is in medical school in Ohio now and I am studying sociology in England, his Milton book on the bookshelf directly next to my bed. We will see each other again when the summer sun is bright in June. I cannot say with absolute certainly that we will spend the rest of our lives together, but I know in that moment of reunion and love, the feeling will wash over us that begs the moment be eternal. From the book he gave me, John Milton's words will swirl in the air . . .

"Love led them on, and Faith who knew them best."
—Milton, Sonnet 14

WRIGHT
Tony and Susan

I wrote a novel. I spent five years working and sweating on that. She knew it. She clearly knew it. She never asked to read it. I'll do it sometime when it is published, she once told me. Maybe it will never be published, I answered. It is very likely, and she knows it.

Months, years passed. A couple of weeks before last Christmas, during one of our silent dinners, she asked me if I saw something in our neighborhood bookshop I would like to read in particular. I answered that I was interested in *Tony and Susan* by Austin Wright. I told her that it is a novel talking about a woman who never cared about reading her husband's unpublished manuscript.

"Oh, cool," she commented. I took her question as something like an investigation to choose a Christmas gift for me.

On December 25, I found *Tony and Susan* under the Christmas tree, wrapped in red paper and with a card: "To my favorite reader, with love." She still hadn't read my manuscript. She still hasn't.

WINTERSON
Art and Lies; Art Objects

The ending was all there, perfectly, months before the years we were together. In the beginning, he was living far away, and this was before email. We wrote real letters and fell in love and began to read the same books at the same time so we could write about them. We agreed to read Jeanette Winterson—well, that was the thing. Over a scratchy phone connection I agreed to read her book of short stories, *Art and Lies,* and he agreed to read her book of essays, *Art Objects.* Our insights began to seem odd and we grew careful in responding. We figured out the original misunderstanding but, sure enough, all kinds of disagreements, careful lies, and deep objections came to light during our terminal stages. But our child is Art enough, and I still treasure the letters.

WALLACE
Infinite Jest

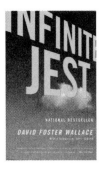

He gave me *Infinite Jest* to read one summer because he told me that after he read it, he felt like he would never need to read anything else ever again. We'd been going out a year. I started it off a little wary of reading a book that would supposedly make me never want to read again. I should have known I would never have the ego to think I didn't need to read.

I got through about thirty pages of it. I liked it, I genuinely did; it was charming but I just knew I would never have the time to finish it. I wanted to focus on school, so I gave it back to him. He lashed out at me and we replayed our favorite argument, like an old record.

He said: You don't love me.
I protested: Yes, I do!
I said: You don't respect me.
He protested: Yes, I do!

A year later I'd finally had it with his disrespect of my mind, of my body. It turns out there's a reason actions speak louder than words: sometimes we lie to each other, and to ourselves, and we don't even know it.

THAYLI
60 Indian Poets

He gave it to me on my twenty-second birthday. My English teacher. The love of my life.

On the flyleaf he wrote, "To a possible good poet from a failed poet."

He had lied. He was a good poet.

But maybe a disastrous muse.

VONNEGUT
Cat's Cradle

We dated in high school when a friend set us up. Both of us were children who didn't know what we wanted; our relationship lasted only a few months. A year later, around Christmastime, when we went our separate ways to separate colleges, we tried it again. This time the relationship lasted years. We became best friends, in love, inseparable. We would try new restaurants. We would have bonfires on the lake. I would visit him every other weekend, and his roommates thought of me as a constant.

But looking back, we were still children who didn't know what we wanted. We tried to want the same things, to force our just-starting lives to go in the same direction. To keep our same friend group in place always. Change was to be feared, avoided, because it was hastening our inevitable breakup.

He wouldn't say that. He would say that the breakup came out of nowhere. A shocking, earth-shattering surprise. That thought still makes me feel a little sad, a little guilty, even all these years later.

I was always attracted by how much he read. Constantly. Everything. He never wanted to voice an opinion of a book or a writer without reading their entire life's work, and he hated not being able to voice an opinion. So, he read. I would read the same books, hoping it would be a conversation starter. The first book he gave me was *Cat's Cradle*. In it—because we were children, because serious things made us both uncomfortable, because we were both still learning how to be in relationships (never mind in a relationship with each other!)—he wrote a funny note in the front about how he promised he bought me this copy new, that he didn't just regift the copy he had bought for himself. He didn't wrap it; he just put a goofy Christmas bow on it.

I miss our friendship every day. We've both moved on; sometimes we see each other for coffee or at a Christmas party in town, but rarely. We usually try small talk for a while, and then sit back and wonder how we are both so different than we used to be, and then we start talking about books again. *Cat's Cradle* and the note in the front seem like a moment frozen in history when there was so much potential between us.

VARIOUS
A Treasury of the World's Best Loved Poems

A woman I was involved with picked this book up for me at a run-down used-book store in Beaufort, South Carolina. However, she apparently "never found the right time" to give it to me, and a few months later we broke up. About a month later I found this book on my bed with a note attached; she had given it to my housemate to give to me. The note was deeply apologetic, optimistic, insincerely cheery and sincerely conciliatory . . . all qualities that, despite being highly admirable, you don't want in a note from your ex shortly after breaking up.

I should also mention that it was my birthday. I know that there was no malicious intent behind this (though I didn't think so at the time), but, needless to say, I was none too happy that she thought this was the long-awaited "right time."

In any case, I was still feeling pretty raw about the whole thing, and as a result, I shelved it and never took the time to look at it. I had considered throwing away the note and giving the book away, but I couldn't bring myself to do it. I almost never part with books and I never throw away letters.

Now that some time has passed and all of the negative feelings I have about her and that relationship have long since vanished, I'm glad that I held on to the book. I still haven't read it (although I read through that note a few more times than was probably healthy) and I have no desire to. It sits on my shelf, unread and collecting dust, an object that, like the relationship, no longer inspires in me pain, regret, or nostalgia. It's a part of my past that simply is, existing for itself and by itself, inert on the bottom shelf.

TOLSTOY
Anna Karenina

We were married. For our anniversary that year he gave me a copy of *Anna Karenina*—a beautiful old copy with soft, pale, unevenly cut pages and a dark cover. I think he thought that since I was "the serious one," I'd appreciate its heft and Russian-ness. I read most of it sitting on our tiny apartment porch trying to ignore him as he practiced his one-man mime show. In context, it seemed to me like a big long story about how staying married to an asshole makes you do dumb things. I filed for divorce three years later.

LAMOTT
Bird by Bird: Some Instructions on Writing and Life

I met my friend, T, about two years ago. I was volunteering at the school where she teaches literacy. From the very get-go I knew she was "my people." We got along famously. It was nice to have someone genuinely excited about my budding career as a novelist. She felt free to share favorite books with me and explained why each intrigued her so. I listened and took notes, finding it insightful to have such an avid reader share what made each book work. In turn, I shared some of my favorite authors with her, and so grew a friendship sparked by the love of books.

One day, as we were chatting in the hallway, I mentioned how I was suffering writer's block in a major way. Normally I wouldn't tell anyone about this. Some people just find it impossible to be encouraging. It's like admitting impotency. It's a failure to do my job. It's embarrassing and humiliating. I knew she would never look down on me, though, so I poured my heart out about how unsure I was of where the book was going, if I was being true to the main character and to myself as a writer, how overwhelming the process is. (This is my sixth novel and it never seems to get any easier.)

Without replying to me, she grabbed one of the students nearby and told her to run up to her classroom and grab a particular book. The student came back with *Bird by Bird*. I told her I really had so many books lined up to read and I didn't want to keep it from her for too long. She put up her hand to stop me and said, "My books are your books. Keep it as long as you need to."

I read several other books I had purchased for research and inspiration and still hadn't moved forward on my own manuscript. I sat staring at my laptop and noticed the book sitting right next to the keyboard. I curled up in my reading chair and read it in about two hours. As soon as I finished the last page, I ran to my laptop and began putting the finishing touches on the novel that had been sitting dormant for so many days . . . after I wrote a heartfelt thank-you email to T, of course.

WATERS
The Night Watch

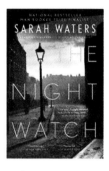

She isn't much for reading. She'll tell you she has honestly read one book front to back of her own free will and enjoyed it. She pokes casual fun at my obsessive reading habits, though she never means any of it. This wasn't the first book she gave me, but it was the first she picked up without me being present to tell her I wanted it. She often jokes about how she never listens to me, but on a visit to her home I was surprised with a copy of this book. She remembered that I love the author and this was the only one at the time I hadn't read and did not own. I was touched by her willingness to brave the bookstore to find it for me and her suggestion that she play on her Game Boy for a while so I could start reading it as we lay entwined on the bed. It meant more to me then she'll ever know, even today, and while we are still together and plan to be for a long time, I don't think I'll ever be able to express it.

KUNDERA
The Unbearable Lightness of Being

She was beautiful, for starters, but also bright. I played sports, and outside of assigned reading in school I had never read a book in my entire life. She put it on my desk at the beginning of summer and asked me to read it. I loved her but didn't think a book could mean so much. I didn't read it. It stayed in the same spot on my desk for the entire summer, until one day the book was gone and so was she. I wished I'd read it sooner. It was too late. I went away to college and studied English literature. I never wanted to miss out on another bright book or beautiful girl again.

STYRON
Sophie's Choice

An ex-girlfriend gave me a copy of *Sophie's Choice* for my birthday. Neither of us had read it, but we both vaguely knew it was about the Holocaust. She decided that it would be a nice personal touch to write little love notes in the margins at random points. Reading it was like reading a completed Mad Libs about genocide, and the blanks told me how I made life worth living. The contrast certainly made the book more emotional. I still have it in a crate somewhere. I think if I reread it, the notes would bring out different emotions now.

GIBRAN
The Prophet

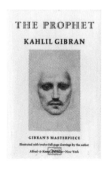

My aunt gave me a copy of *The Prophet* as part of her gift for my high school graduation. I read it eagerly, wide-eyed, hopeful. Sentimental, as I am. Later, I decided it was too hippy-ish and relegated it to the back of my shelves. Later still, I opened it back up and saw that it contained much more wisdom than I'd ever given it credit for. Like my grandpa (her dad) says, "young and dumb."

STODDARD
The High House

He didn't give me a copy; I doubt he had one, and he was certainly too cheap to buy one. I don't remember that he ever gave me a gift he had purchased. Rather, he insisted I read it—that it was the best book he'd ever read, that he thought it was incredibly important. I was three hours away and carless, and I wanted to feel close to him, and I worked at the library, so it was no trouble to find it.

When I did, I was enthralled—slightly appalled by some appropriation of well-beloved characters, but still enchanted by the labyrinthine House and its endless potential. It turned out that the things he liked about it were totally different from the things I liked. I can't even remember what they were now. I was disappointed and didn't read the recommended sequel. I wasn't so wise when, after breaking up with him, I started dating him again six months later. There was no potential in that choice.

The labyrinthine image and the infinite possibilities of the book have stayed with me far longer than any other part of the relationship, and they are some of the concepts I now value most.

POE
The Poe Reader

One of my most vivid childhood memories is of my grandfather and me reading Edgar Allan Poe together. Spending countless nights memorizing "The Raven" and "The Bells" until I could recite them back to him. This was our special bond. None of his other grandchildren loved reading quite like he did. When his health kept him from traveling, he gave me my own copy of *The Poe Reader* to keep so I could continue to read Poe's stories even if we weren't together. Even though I'm older now and he has left this world, I still pick up the book he gave me from time to time, scanning the pages and rereading our favorites. My own special way of remembering a great man who taught me my love for books.

BAUM
The Oz Books

My uncle, B. H., gave me his childhood set of Oz books when I was in my early teens. I ended up reading most of those written by Baum. This was my first book series and an introduction to fantasy. It taught me that when you find an author you like, you should stick with him or her!

BRADFORD
Red Sky at Morning

My dad has given me many great books over the years—*Pride and Prejudice, Zen and the Art of Motorcycle Maintenance,* and the Harry Potter series, to name a few. The best one he ever gave me, his all-time favorite, was *Red Sky at Morning* by Richard Bradford. It's an absolutely perfect coming of age novel set in rural New Mexico. It came out before there was really a YA market, but it made me a lover of teen lit. It's no coincidence that I'm now a YA librarian in rural New Mexico. Something about the book struck a deep chord in me.

Both Dad and I continue to reread *Red Sky at Morning* regularly. As a kid, I worshiped my dad, but as an adult we have kind of a strained relationship. However, that shared language of a book we both know backward and forward is a thread that always binds us and a special secret language. Corazón Sagrado is our real hometown, as a family.

GOREY
Amphigorey

My parents were devout balletomanes; they followed Balanchine's career closely and spent decades attending the New York City Ballet. At every performance they shared the audience with a striking fellow with a beard, strange-looking jewelry, and sneakers, sporting an ankle-length fur coat. They made inquiries and soon discovered that this fellow was a Mr. Edward Gorey: writer, artist, and illustrator of books. They were captivated.

I was one of those withdrawn, silent kids, and I lived in a world of my own. I was also a voracious reader, and the nineteenth century seemed much more real to me than the twentieth. All my heroes and imaginary friends were long gone: Oscar Wilde, Charlotte Brontë, Ambrose Bierce, Edgar Allen Poe. I had trouble relating to much of the squalid, technicolor brouhaha of the late twentieth century, and I struggled somewhat to find a vision of the world that was both comforting and familiar.

One day my parents brought me a book entitled *Amphigorey,*

and on the title page I found my name beautifully inscribed in a banner. I was very young and had never seen Edward Gorey's work before. The moment I laid eyes on that book, however, I knew I had found a muse: here was a world that finally made sense—beautifully, fascinatingly so. I read and reread every story in that book, but I was most captivated with a tale told only in images: "The West Wing." I knew that I had found the tone with which I wanted to live. It was a strange epiphany to have as a young child, but there it is. I hunted down and devoured every Gorey book I could find. I entered Gorey's timeless, whimsical, droll, and wicked world, and I never left.

The years passed; I spent my time making music and holding meaningless day jobs until my health gave way, at which point I decided that my days remaining on this Earth should be spent beautifully. I became a professional aesthete and antiques dealer and created the world in which I now live. When I finally found a little Second Empire Victorian home, I concentrated on creating the perfect library. One of the very first things I hung up in that room was an Edward Gorey artist's proof (a rather whimsical bat). In this home I allow nonsensical objects to play with one another, and I still dream of a house large enough to contain rooms with nothing but one giant urn, an upturned chair, or a curious sofa . . .

My parents' gift of *Amphigorey* was a significant childhood event. I recently asked my father what had prompted that gift all those years ago (and why they had had it autographed). He replied that Edward Gorey had seemed like an interesting fellow, and since I already lived in a world of my own, they thought I'd like some company.

A greater gift can hardly be imagined.

TOLKIEN
The Children of Húrin

My dad and I have never had a very close relationship, as fathers and daughters go. He was a pilot for twenty years, and so most of my childhood memories of him are of him leaving for long trips to places whose names I could barely pronounce. He would bring me sand roses from Saudi Arabia, strange currency from Moscow, wooden carvings of exotic women from India that still smell like sandalwood, and dolls from China that I couldn't play with for fear of breaking their delicate paper parasols.

On the rare nights that he was home we would sit on our ratty blue couch and read from his twenty-year-old copy of *The Lord of the Rings*. My bedtime stories were the epic adventures of hobbits, elves, and men. I had nightmares about Shelob when I was six years old that completely exasperated my mother, but my dad insisted it would build character.

Over the years I realized that trinkets from Africa and Europe do not a father make, and began to harbor a lot of resentment. I didn't talk to my father for a long time. The year I graduated from high school he gave me a special edition of *The Children of Húrin,* by Tolkien. Inside he had written: "Always imagine. Always dream."

I am about to graduate from college with a degree in literature and I still blame him for my enduring love of stories, and the value of eloquent expression of universal human emotion. He gave me this copy of *The Children of Húrin,* and so much more.

MARTIN
The Battle of the Frogs and the Mice

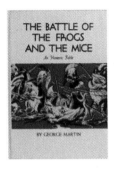

I wasn't so much given this book as I absconded with it. I didn't know where my mother had gotten it, but it was kept carefully hidden from me under stacks of towels in the hall bathroom linen closet: maybe it was too violent or just too bizarre for a picture book. It was there for years and years, never moved (maybe she'd forgotten about it) until I finally took it and put it on the bookshelf in my bedroom. She never mentioned it, and maybe she never saw it in its new location, but I treasure it, perhaps because it's violent and bizarre, and I wish I could finance a reprinting.

And just maybe she only had it in the first place because Herman Munster (actor Fred Gwynne) had illustrated it . . .

SMITH, ZADIE
On Beauty

He was my best friend. He was sensitive and honest. I was delusional and precarious. There were many things wrong with the relationship, which, of course, made us right for each other. Over the years he gave me many, many books. Some were just okay and others were truly beautiful. Each book, I thought, held some encrypted key, some form of insight, to our relationship.

After a slow and painful process, we ended our relationship. I moved away to start graduate school with my current partner (who never gives me books). While unpacking my books, I saw the copy of *On Beauty* he gave me. Inside it said:

> *L—*
> *You could definitely be an English professor.*
> *—D. P.*

I'd forgotten that he inscribed all the books he gave me. He believed in my dream before I did. I wish I had believed in us.

SMITH, LANE
It's a Book

He, libertarian lawyer—(I was being open-minded, nonjudgmental. He was smart, even if I thought some of his beliefs were essentially inhumane)—defended good-naturedly his beloved Kindle. I am a devotee of the written word, of the printed page. Books are real. The speed with which we get through them is not relevant, and increasing that speed has never been a goal of mine. I only ask that time expand to let me read more, not that books contract to let me gulp them down faster.

But he read, at least, and I am not a geek-ogre. He spoke of a gift he'd ordered for me, and one day when I was at his apartment, it arrived in its box from Amazon. I turned my back while he unwrapped it.

"It's a book!" he exclaimed. And so it was. *It's a Book,* by Lane Smith, in which an ape, a donkey (read: jackass), and a mouse learn all about the differences between old-style paper and high-tech e-formats. It was a book. That much, at least, he understood.

SLANG

He gave me a slang dictionary for my some-teenth birthday. At the time I thought it was stupid and easy. Out of all the books he could have chosen, it was the kind displayed in the checkout line. I never read it and, years later, have discovered it's gone, lost in the cosmos of forty-seven search pages on Barnesandnoble.com.

It is also only now that I realize its simple thoughtfulness, the sort that really captured us in our years of growing up together. The gift was the ideal combination of my love of books and his love of silliness. But this discovery came far too late. For, of course, we never did speak the same language. And it proved impossible to find a dictionary of ourselves for the other.

SALINGER
Franny and Zooey

He was handsome and sweet but not much of a reader. I gave him my (much cherished) copy of *Franny and Zooey,* telling him how much the book had meant to me growing up. He seemed happy, so I followed with others I thought he'd like. But when he moved in some months later, bringing with him a box of smelly secondhand paperbacks of the kind the library practically begs you to take off their hands, there was no sign of *Franny and Zooey* or any of the other books I'd shared with him from my collection.

He told me they must have been "accidentally" thrown out during the move. To add insult to injury, he insisted his ragtag books sit on the shelf alongside mine. I dumped the illiterate cad not long after.

SHAKESPEARE
Henry V

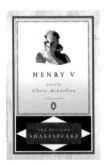

We were a library, she and I, loving and sharing literature. I thought it would be forever, but it lasted only three weeks. I couldn't renew our relationship.

At the naive age of twenty-one, and in four college English classes, I was drowning in books. That is, until she came along and saved me with Shakespeare. She approached me one day after our seminar and put her freshly painted nails on my shoulder. I looked up and put my book down. She asked what I was reading. I held up *The Woman Warrior*. She smiled, and so did I.

One week and a date later, we exchanged books. She gave me her annotated copy of *Henry V* and I lent her my new copy of *The Miraculous Journey of Edward Tulane*. I leafed through her book that night, ignoring the text. The green cover had her perfume, and the aroma of paper acidity wafted through my room. Inside, her handwriting was cursive and bold and strangely beautiful. I went over the words with my fingers, rubbing the letters, feeling the curves. I touched "lust" and felt it warm on my lips. I touched "death" and imagined my heart stopping. Her words were like Braille—and I was blind.

We drank coffee the next week and discussed our books. It was intellectual heaven. I was beginning to understand why people fell in love. It was for this. To talk about metaphors and plot twists while holding hands. To eat raspberry pastries while laughing about Shakespeare's double entendres. To read in bed with the one you love.

On the third week she dropped the seminar. She had told me it wasn't interesting anymore. I didn't inquire much. She wanted to change to a different class. I supported her choice. We promised to still meet afterward, or before her new class. There wasn't any time. She later got a full-time job and I struggled to keep up with the readings.

After a month of failed attempts at meeting up, I ended it. I kept her copy of *Henry V*. On occasion, I look at her handwriting to see if it still has the same effect on me. And it does.

SPOTO
The Art of Alfred Hitchcock

During our first year of marriage my wife gave me *The Art of Alfred Hitchcock* by Donald Spoto. I had just started getting into classic movies, and Alfred Hitchcock was my new favorite director. At the time it seemed like the perfect gift for someone who had a new hobby, nothing more and nothing less. She can't have known how this book would impact my life. It seems silly to say that a book about movies can be life changing, but there can be no other way to describe it. Not only did it give me insight on my new favorite director, but it opened me up to a whole new way of thinking about movies and how movies have the power to speak to people and make a difference in their lives. The book also taught me to pay attention to every little detail in movies, because nothing is wasted in a movie. It all has significance.

However, the greatest gift the book has given me is hours and hours of conversation with my wife. After watching a movie and reading the corresponding chapter together, we can sit for hours and discuss the various meanings in the movie. Eventually the conversation usually shifts back to our own lives and relationship. Those long conversations are priceless and very meaningful to me. I will forever treasure them.

After reading the book cover to cover and multiple viewings of the Hitchcock movies, I use the book now as a guide or reference work to remind me how to watch movies. Every once in a while, though, I will convince my wife to watch "one of those boring classics" and read one of those "long philosophical chapters" with ulterior motives.

SCHLINK
The Reader

I picked up a used copy of this at a book sale on campus, thinking fondly of the movie, and set it back down upon realizing I was short on cash. When I returned home to my then-boyfriend, I told him about it and how silly it was of me to forget to put it on a reserve list.

The next day he surprised me with the exact same book, having driven to my campus to track it down and buy it for me. I read it and loved it, and loved him, too, I'm sure. It was a habit of his to trail after me at bookstores, take note of the books I wanted but couldn't afford, and then return in secret to buy them as gifts for me every month. He'd then listen happily as I talked about the books, as if my reading them was enough for the both of us.

He was very sweet to me, and what we had was good, but when the relationship fell apart in a horrible manner and I was beating myself up over it, someone pointed out that the next person I dated would probably read the books before giving them to me. You know, a reader.

WELSH
Trainspotting

About a month after we met I went to visit a friend in San Francisco, and while I was away, Irvine Welsh was doing a signing at a local bookstore. My friend and I both shared a love of all things UK, including *Trainspotting*. Since I was out of town, he arranged with my sister to come by and pick up my copy of *Trainspotting* and get it signed by the author for me. He surprised me with it when I got back from my trip, and still to this day, it was one of the most thoughtful things anyone has ever done for me.

In the end, and after a year and a half, our relationship didn't work out, but we managed to stay close and he's still one of my best friends. He always did me right, and I've promised myself to always be as good to him as he has been to me. It's not often you get the chance to make friends like this.

RUSSELL
The Sparrow; Children of God

The first and last books he ever gave me were Mary Doria Russell's *The Sparrow* and its sequel, *Children of God*.

When he gave me *The Sparrow*, I was twenty-two and we had just started dating. He had been a philosophy major, and I had somewhat reluctantly gone corporate after college. I loved the idea that he thought about big, important ideas while I slaved away at a desk job. He captured my heart with the unspoken promise that we'd always intellectually engage with each other over the books we read and that, with him and through our discussions, I could keep my love of literature alive even while working for The Man. I envisioned finding and sharing books with each other for the rest of our lives. Probably reading them in front of roaring fires in the winter, too. I was so young and naive and full of hope for the future and what love could mean that I would have believed just about anything. Turned out to be a classic case of bait and switch. Very quickly after I got in too deep to get out, he stopped reading. And

I don't just mean he stopped reading books with big, important ideas. He stopped reading, period. Barely even a magazine here and there for eleven years. He had read enough books before we met to give the illusion of being well read while I was falling in love with him, but not enough to last even six months beyond that.

He gave me *Children of God* for my thirty-third birthday. Not because he had found it and thought I might like it, but because I specifically told him to buy it for me. I think I was hoping he'd read it after I did and we'd talk about it, like we had *The Sparrow*. I knew our marriage was failing even if he didn't, and I guess I wanted to recapture some of the magic. He showed absolutely no interest in reading it or even discussing it with me. Six months later I filed for divorce.

I am now with an admitted nonreader who was very upfront about this aspect of his identity from the beginning.

WALTERS; LOUX
Clean Food; The Balanced Plate

We grew up together, same schools, same classes, but were never friends. I had a crush on him in the first grade and have warm, vivid memories of both him and his mother picking him up from school. We ran into each other in Penn Station a few years ago and started dating soon after. His parents loved good food as well as cooking, and knew I did as well. For Christmas, both he and his mother gave me cookbooks. He gave me *Clean Food*, by Terry Walters, which at the time I remember thinking was sweet but, once I looked at the recipes, realized was a lazy choice on his part— bare bones recipes with little imagination. His mother, however, gave me a copy of Renee Loux's *The Balanced Plate*, a much more detailed, insightful, and delicious-recipe-filled cookbook. He left me a few months later. I still think of his mother every time I use the cookbook, and I miss her.

RECLAM VERLAG
Various

The books they gave me were yellow. They were Reclam classics: Goethe, Lessing, Schiller, Brecht, Sophocles, to be read for school, according to the *Lehrplan*. No pleading with the teacher; no escape from those pages. Reading the books often proved to be an exercise in endurance: five more pages to the next chapter, four more pages, three more pages, two more pages, one more page, next chapter, fifteen more pages . . .

Yet, in memory, all those yellow books merged into one or, rather, into one huge stage. I can hardly remember the quotes we marked in class to refer to in exams, but the characters are still present: Nathan, Faust, Antigone, Saladin, Mutter Courage, Mephistopheles, Tell—talking in verse, in lines noted in distant times and places that—unfolding in yellow—became a part of my world, book by book.

ROWLING
Harry Potter and the Philosopher's Stone

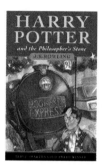

Only he could have guessed that I was still a child inside.

Never in my wildest dreams did I imagine that someday I'd fall for a fantasy novel. I always considered myself past the age for children's fiction; realistic fiction is my cup of tea.

Graham Greene hath said, "Perhaps it is only in childhood that books have any deep influence on our lives . . . What do we ever get nowadays from reading to equal the excitement and the revelation in those first fourteen years?" I, too, had my moments of "excitement and revelation" as a fourteen-year-old: the Secret Seven and the Famous Five series, *Alice's Adventures in Wonderland, Kidnapped* et al. These books had done wonders for my imagination. But was it possible for me to undergo a similar "excitement" after the age of fourteen? It was. In my case, this book almost proved Greene wrong.

The Hogwarts School of Witchcraft and Wizardry caught me off guard. My first encounter with "The Letters from No One" and

"The Keeper of the Keys," my first walk through Diagon Alley, the first mind-boggling search for Platform Nine and Three-quarters, and the first meeting with Ron and Hermione still lie fresh in my memory. An "unbreakable vow" was made. I'd read all the Potter books, come what may, and the magical bond was thus sealed.

He taught me one thing—it's never too late to begin. I bought the remaining six books myself, though. That's the problem with childhood friends. They know you far too well. He borrowed the remaining six books of the series from me. He never bought books for himself. He bought them only for me.

All of Voldemort's horcruxes might have been discovered and destroyed, but my seven horcruxes still remain safe on my bookshelf.

The World Book Encyclopedia

During Christmas 1984, most ten-year-old boys were excited about getting *Thriller* on vinyl, Atari games, or Transformers. And I did receive my fair share of standard loot. But the best gift I received was a set of *World Book* 1984 encyclopedias.

Up until then, I had enjoyed reading through every one of my mom's *Golden Book* encyclopedias from her own childhood. Since they were from 1960, I was in danger of believing nothing important had happened since then. My family united to address this risk by giving my brother and me the 1984 edition of *World Book* encyclopedias. My parents, grandparents, and, most notably, aunt Emma all pitched in. If Emma ever gave me a gift that was not a book, I have no memory of it.

The encyclopedias started arriving, one letter at a time. As each one arrived, I read it, cover to cover, before the next one arrived. But Aunt Emma had grander designs. Every time she called my mom, she had a question for me to research in the encyclopedias. I was to discuss my findings by the end of the call. I now suspect this was a way to keep me occupied while Emma and Mom caught up, but at the time it was a chance for this know-it-all to prove he knew it all.

The exercises weren't just isolated fact checking. She didn't ask us the population of Seattle. She asked instead, "Which city has a larger population: Seattle or San Francisco?" No-brainer! San Francisco's a huge city, right? It had the gold rush, it's in California—isn't it clearly the bigger of the two?

I checked the *World Book*. What? Seattle's twice the size? "How is that possible?" I asked Emma when I reported back. She told me San Francisco's region had more people, but the city itself had no room to grow either out (because it's at the tip of a peninsula) or up (because the earthquakes make people leery of putting up tall buildings).

In this one exercise, I had learned not just facts, but how they related to each other. I had learned that facts are meaningless without context: Seattle and San Francisco were both big, but they were different kinds of big. And I had learned that I should be wary of assumptions like the one I had made. I learned that facts and knowledge are not understanding, and understanding is not wisdom. Books aren't just for absorbing; they are for thinking. The gift of a book is really an attempt at a gift of thinking, and Emma made sure the gift achieved its goal.

WYNDHAM
The Day of the Triffids

My dad has never been great with gifts. Not to say there haven't been many that I've really appreciated, but almost all were taken directly off the lists he asked me to provide every birthday and Christmas. Books were the one exception. Every gift-giving holiday I received two books—one I had asked for, and one that I hadn't. The latter were never remarkable until the summer I turned eleven and he introduced me to science fiction. It was a bold move given that my only previous interaction with the genre was falling asleep during every Star Wars movie, but I read *The Day of the Triffids* and fell in love. I slowly acquired all of Wyndham's novels—some as gifts, others on my own—and moved on to H. G. Wells, Madeleine L'Engle, John Christopher, Orson Scott Card, Philip K. Dick, Bradbury, Vonnegut, Orwell, and many more. My collection is still growing and I have him to thank (though this past Christmas book was written by a TV comedian).

NABOKOV
Lolita

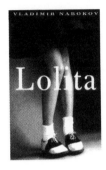

I was nineteen.
He was thirty.
I'm not sure he thought
this gift through.

DYLAN & ROGERS
Forever Young

I took calculus that summer. The class met in the mornings, filling the humid hours before noon with integrals and chalk dust.

In the afternoons, I worked in the studio office of a small community journal, brewing muddy coffee in the pot balanced in the windowsill, stapling thick copies that stamped my palms blue with ink print. There was no air conditioner, just a rusty fan that spluttered and cussed. I would sweat through my gray pencil skirt, moistening the vinyl chair with the soft pattern of my thighs.

In the evenings, I drove an hour to meet Chuck. Chuck's legal name was Oscar and he worked as the accountant for a local mortuary. I imagined his careful tabulations, sheets of numbers and figures, stacked amid fat syringes of embalming fluid. Given his prowess with numbers, he tutored me in calculus, every Monday, Tuesday, and Wednesday at the library near his home.

My birthday that summer fell on a Tuesday, so my mom met me halfway between work and my appointment with Chuck. We chose a Chinese restaurant, ordering cucumbers with vinegar and vegetable dumplings steamed and delivered in a wicker basket.

She gave me this book; unwrapped, handed over the table. And though I was turning eighteen, though she said little, if anything, to explain or contextualize its presence at my birthday dinner . . . I understood.

May you build a ladder to the stars / And climb on every rung . . .

I just needed a reminder. A children's book. Something to let me know that, on the eighteenth anniversary of my birth, I could be, if I so chose, forever young.

HEMON
The Lazarus Project

My mom is a retired high school English teacher. We are both huge readers but have always had very different taste in books. I know that calling something "very" different is often considered a grammatical faux pas—two things are either different or they aren't—but I believe it applies here, because our interests are indeed that estranged, which is surprising since we both love literary fiction, usually of the same narrow level (we read what's new, what's buzzy, what's being reviewed everywhere).

In my senior year of college, my mother turned sixty. Although it meant missing Halloween partying on campus (it always did; her birthday is November 1), I drove to an inn some hours away, in Dover, Vermont, to meet up with the rest of my family and spend the weekend together. On Saturday we all drove into town and found a charming bookstore. Inside, on one of the display tables, they had an autographed copy of *The Lazarus Project* by Aleksandar Hemon. It was a new book that I knew I had heard mentioned somewhere but couldn't recall anything about. I had also never read anything by Hemon. But the striking, pretty cover and the description was enough to get me excited. I spent a lot of time with it, then moved on, and then we all left the bookstore. Later, back at the inn, my mom took it out and gave it to me; she must have seen me looking at it and gone back to buy it when we all split up and went into different shops. There was no big significant moment. I was appreciative and started reading it right away. But that night, after we gave Mom her gifts and ate dinner in the dining room, I brought the book to her and asked her to write a note in it, like she used to when I was little. She wrote, as is her style, something warm and loving but not too verbose. I don't even recall exactly what it was. There wasn't any occasion to reference (what would she write, "Happy birthday to me, D! Love, Mom"?), and her note was brief. The book is now on my shelf at home, and I haven't even reread it (yet) since that first feverish reading (it was, of course, a terrific novel). Even more in support of the book deserving no significance in my giant library is that I know the note inside of it is a bit artificial, in the sense that I requested it be written.

And yet, I've now read more by Hemon, so any time I come across his name, I think of that book sitting on my shelf at home, and of the experience of the weekend in Vermont, and of my mom buying it for me and inscribing it. I think of the book whenever I see autographed copies of books on display in stores, and even whenever I see a truly appealing, interesting-looking hardcover novel. And I haven't asked my mom to write a note in a book for me since then, and I likely won't ask again, so it may be the last book in which she ever writes me a note. And that's one of many qualities that make the book feel special to me and makes it stand out from the many other books that my mom bought me (*Indignation*, *The Thousand Autumns of Jacob de Zoet*) or lent me (*Never Let Me Go*, *Great Expectations*). It feels to me like the kind of object that, decades from now (I hope many decades), when my mom is gone and I cannot talk with her about books anymore, I will cherish and keep somewhere important, separate from the rest of my books.

MOORE
Absolute Watchmen

So I gave my high school sweetheart *Absolute Watchmen* for our two-year anniversary (two years as boyfriend and girlfriend, I was young—it was a big deal). When we broke up, I was upset. Not only because we broke up, but because I wanted this limited edition copy back. It was a hard find and I knew he didn't appreciate it as much as I did. I told my then "just a friend" about it in the midst of my crisis. He comforted me and assured me that I'd find another copy some time soon. I thought nothing of it, but knew he was right as he urged me to not talk to my ex, no matter how awesome the book.

A couple months later it was Christmas Eve. Me and my "just a friend" went for a car ride to check out all the Christmas lights around town. On the floor in the passenger seat was a gift wrapped in old newspaper comics. I held it, and before I even took a moment to unwrap it, I knew exactly what it was by its size and weight. My "just a friend" turned out to be my best friend, and eventually, my boyfriend.

That was years ago. We broke up a few months ago, but I still have my copy of *Absolute Watchmen* this time. I look at that copy and know that no matter what happens between us, my limited edition *Watchmen* is safe on my shelf. It reminds me of how beautiful we were and how lucky I am to have such good friends, even in our times apart.

PLATH
The Collected Poems

The day I left for college you slipped it into the backseat of my car. I'd wanted it for months. And now the well-thumbed book sits on the part of my shelf I save for the books I love most, with your inscription in red pen; your beautiful, slim handwriting; your assurances that I am meant to write, that I should use the book not as means of negative comparison but as means of reminding me that this, *this,* is what I am supposed to do. I am almost out of college; I didn't want to, could never unwrap me from you.

GAIMAN
The Sandman Vol. 9: The Kindly Ones

We never wrote each other letters. We never bought each other books. We were both very talented and very busy. Torn between school and the family he was starting, we didn't have time for letters. We both loved to read, especially Neil Gaiman's works. So we took quotes from *The Sandman* and scattered them over the Internet. Those were our letters, our I-love-you's. After he left, it took years for me to pick up any of Gaiman's novels. I still consider him my Morpheus, my lost dream.

> "I don't remember what you smell like. You've been gone two days, and I don't remember how you smelled. You didn't smell like anyone else. I like the way you smelled. I . . . I miss you a lot."
> —Hob Gadling, *The Kindly Ones*

WALLER
The Bridges of Madison County

She had shared far better books with me. The kind that equally inspire and boil jealousy in budding novelists. I read every one, pausing to linger in all the sentences we both would have underlined. Books were our conversation.

But that day in the coffeeshop she was holding *The Bridges of Madison County*. We'd both read it years before. We felt a little embarrassed about that. Still, I would read it one more time.

She smiled a sad, sweet smile and slid the book across the table. It made a sound like a sigh. Then she left without a word to meet her husband for lunch.

RILKE
The Book of Images

On a rainy morning as I hurriedly made my way to work, a guy approached me and asked for my phone number. I obliged. We were both temporarily back in our native country for career endeavors and had taken up residence in the same apartment building.

It was the first and only time in my life that I allowed myself to come so frighteningly close to a beautiful stranger who, within hours of conversation that spanned one evening and a sunrise, revealed himself to be that mythical, wondrous, intelligent guy I had dreamed up in my head all these years. There he was, my elusive prototype, dreamed into real human-flesh existence. How could such a thrilling moment have been born out of the simple arbitrary act of asking for one's phone number?

Somewhere in between those hours of talk on our shared love for travel, long walks, airports, and a habit of writing in journals emerged the inevitable deal-breaker question about who our favorite poet was, and instantly that magical lock-and-key fit clicked into place with Rainer Maria Rilke. That immediately drew me to him as it spoke of the depth of his appreciation for the virtues of solitude, longing, and beauty in its utmost simplicity—themes that only Rilke has the profound eloquence for. Every word and action exchanged thereafter was steeped in drunken gladness and a silent triumph for having found a piece of myself in another. I had become painfully aware that the fraction of time and space I was sharing with this amazing guy in every ticking second that passed until dawn was really just a dream that I had to wake up from eventually. I surrendered myself to the dream.

That dawn morning was the last time I expected to see him. I didn't ask for his last name or his email address. In two days I would fly away and return to my permanent country of work and, perhaps because we both knew I was leaving soon, our time together felt rare and sacred. The next day, as I packed up and got ready to check out of my apartment and leave, he asked if he could see me before I left. We met briefly, and in those final minutes before parting he gave me his own tattered, earmarked copy of *The Book of Images* by Rilke with an inscription at the front that will hold me eternally captive to the memory of who he is and what we shared that night. There was no way I could escape him now. I kept this book on my bedside for months and it lay there like a living presence that stood guard over my joyful nights of sleep, dreaming of beautiful possibilities uttered in exquisite Rilkean verse. Never has a book infused such feverish hope of a romance that could exist, did exist, than this book he gave me.

SMITH
Just Kids

I'm a proud New Yorker . . . he's an expat from Ireland.

We had been dating for a few months and as an innocent Christmas present I gave him *Just Kids* by Patti Smith. It is one of my favorite books; not only because her prose is remarkable, but because she writes about the New York before my time—the New York that I find endlessly fascinating. I wrote a similar yet more personal note in the copy I gave him.

He broke up with me two nights ago in a despicable way. I replayed one of the conversations we'd had in my rumpled bed:

"I started reading *Just Kids,*" he said, with a tone indicating that he was less than pleased with it.

"Well, you just started it," I replied. "This isn't a happy book; it's about the struggle for what you believe in, in the city that you believe in."

"I guess . . ."

"Just give it a chance."

This conversation foreshadowed our future, a mere two days later. If you don't want to put in the work for something or someone you believe in, then I'm glad to be rid of you. Now get out of my damn city.

KIPFER
14,000 Things to be Happy About

14,000
things
to be
happy
about.

THE HAPPY BOOK BY BARBARA ANN KIPFER

He bought this for me in the university bookshop freshman year, and we read it together, giggling under the covers in his dorm room and underlining certain items. The book portrayed a certain WASPy vision of a future I thought I wanted. Perfect days on Martha's Vineyard, Add-A-Bead pearl necklaces, crisp monogrammed shirts . . . that wasn't me. I only thought it was.

Eventually we split up. I think he still has this book, with one significant item underlined: "One perfect lover in college." I guess that's what he was.

ROMEO & ROMEO
11,002 Things to be Miserable About

His new girlfriend
is much more cheerful
than I am.

ROBBINS
Jitterbug Perfume

He told me this was his favorite book. I thought that it meant he believed in eternal love, something that can withstand age and mortality. After all, he also made an offhand romantic comment during one of our first dates about how he bet that we would be married one day.

But in retrospect, while he wanted to be a romantic and an adventurer, he was too wrapped up in fantasy and fiction to pay attention to the reality of life and love. He reveled in the adventure of instability and fleeting pleasures, failing to notice that, unlike the characters in this novel, we were aging and I wanted more than just sex and an occasional meal together. We inevitably ended, and I realize that he probably loved this book not because he believed in real true love, but because all he really wanted was a fun adventure and I was just along for the ride.

BUKOWSKI
Ham on Rye

We were never lovers, but there was something. An interest. Not quite a spark, but more a quiet heat that seemed ready to flare up at any moment, and yet never did. I admired him, his devotion to music and classical guitar and the way he wore his curly hair long.

We went on one date, to a movie. Afterwards we went in separate cars back to his house, and he showed me where he was working on his final project for his music master's degree, then offered me a beer. I awkwardly declined, as I don't drink, and it wasn't long after that that I excused myself and went home. We hadn't even kissed or even really touched.

Some time after that I was diagnosed with cancer and hospitalized. He came to visit me, and when he did, he gave me a copy of *Ham on Rye*. At the time I couldn't focus properly on reading, so it wasn't until many months later, when I was out of the hospital and in remission, that I finally read the book.

It was a depressing time in my life. I had learned that due to damage from chemotherapy, I likely couldn't ever have children. I was depressed and wondered why I had lived.

Reading the book made me even more depressed, and I wondered why in the world he had given it to me.

By that point I had met the man who is now my husband, and due to my new job and going back to school, I didn't see my ex again until after I was already married, years later. We happened to meet at a bookstore, and all the awkwardness came rushing back. I asked him out for coffee, even though I don't drink coffee, because I wanted to ask him about the book. But he gently replied that he was there with his significant other. Embarrassed, I retreated, and I haven't seen him since.

It's been thirteen years since he gave me the book, and much more than cancer and infertility has happened in my life. Now I think I might finally understand what he was trying to say when he gave the book to me.

I think he might have been saying: All that suffering you're going through? It doesn't matter. You can still find joy.

Thank you. I did.

RIMBAUD
Rimbaud Complete

I was just on the cusp of turning eighteen when you gave me *Rimbaud Complete*. You had brought the book to one of our summer book club meetings, and I all but jumped on it.

This was not the first book you gave me—the first was Knowles' *A Separate Peace*, the novel that taught me one can never own too many books, and that one can never mark up a book too much. This is the book that taught me to be reckless, to love with absolute abandon and to take pride in doing so. Yes, you taught me in the classroom for two years, but my most valuable lessons from you have been the ones about life—when to let go, how to be young, how to take care of myself, how to take care of others. As I am writing this, the words you gave me with this book still resonate, even though it's almost been two years:

Rimbaud will be good for you. He was good for me when I turned eighteen (years ago, an old friend gave me a copy of his early work; it tickles me that I was able to return the favor). Read a few of his poems every single day (try to do it outside—I read them by a river near my old house, and the experience was transcendental). He is, at times, capricious, whimsical, pensive, crude, rude, and playful; yet, at all times, he is deliberate and beautiful.

He held the chamber of his heart with furious aggression and vivacity, and he embodied all that is pure, youthful, and energetic. He carried the pulse of life in the veins of his words.

It is your time to feel this same pulse. Jump in; be foolish; be free.

Thank you, Mr. F.

LAWRENCE & LEE
Inherit the Wind

I met him at a political conference. We were both tremendous lovers of American history and we both did theater in high school. He lived three hours away from me, but with the help of Skype, texting, and Facebook, we were able to talk about everything. Our conversations always gravitated towards what books we were reading, and I mentioned that I had wanted to read *Inherit the Wind*. He sent it to me for my birthday, but asked me to wait until he could find time to see me, so we could read it and pretend that we were performing onstage together. He finally came to my house to see me, but as luck would have it, there was a snowstorm that caused a power outage. We read it out loud together by candlelight underneath a warm blanket.

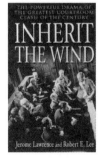

He came out to me when the storm was over. We're still friends.

DISNEY
Beauty and the Beast

As the eldest in a family of five children, my parents couldn't give me books I asked for. Still, I counted myself lucky because I had aunts and uncles who were happy to oblige when my parents could not.

I was six years old when my uncle Joey promised we would buy a hardbound copy of *Beauty and the Beast*. The promised day came—it was a Saturday—but before I could even get ready for the trip to the store, my uncle said we couldn't go. As a child, I hated it when adults didn't keep promises. I cried, and Uncle Bo, who was Uncle Joey's elder brother, asked me to stop. After I had calmed down, he offered to take me to the store and buy the book with him.

When we got the book, I thanked and gave him a kiss. We went to the fast food restaurant next to the bookstore for spaghetti and burgers. It was the first and last time he took me out alone, without my elder cousin, whom he loved to spoil. It was also the first and last book he gave me personally, as I ended up buying books with a credit card he gave me years later, when I was in university.

I got hooked on Sweet Valley books at some point and the hardbound *Beauty and the Beast* went to a shelf where we kept photo albums. If the other adults were pleased with my new obsession, my uncle Bo was not. He finally cracked when I flunked a math test in the third grade, and in his fury, grabbed my growing collection of Sweet Valley paperbacks and hid them. He eventually gave them back, but I resented him for what he did.

A few months after Uncle Bo died in 2008, we cleared our house to prepare for a renovation. Somewhere under the books I had collected over the years, I found my old, battered copy of *Beauty and the Beast*. I separated it from the volumes of Sweet Valley paperbacks and put it in a box with books I read in the university. When boys from the junk shop made their rounds and passed by our house, I sold the whole Sweet Valley collection for ten pesos.

I gave my copy of *Beauty and the Beast* to my elder cousin's daughter, and promised to give her more.

SEUSS
Oh, the Places You'll Go!

Most fourteen-year-olds want a new dirt bike or the latest video game console when the phrase "graduation present" is being thrown around. My older brother got a brand-new bike when he graduated from eighth grade. I received just one book when I graduated, and it changed my life. For my eighth grade graduation my parents bought me *Oh, the Places You'll Go!* by Dr. Seuss.

The day I graduated I remember sitting on the floor in my cap and gown reading it and reminding myself that I would be going somewhere. It was my inspiration. Whenever times got tough, I would pick it up as a reminder to remember that sometimes life would knock me down. Four years later, when I graduated from high school, I mimicked what I had done before. I sat down and read the book, reminding myself that life is a journey. I even kept a quote in my pocket to read up at the pulpit.

So many times in life I've been battered down, but I have learned to celebrate all the moments because they make us who we are. Seuss is my muse and inspiration of sorts, and one simple book transformed my life.

I have yet to graduate from college, but I know that when I do, I'll do the same thing I've done in the past.

BROWN
The Runaway Bunny

You weren't around much when I was little. Always busy—first with the Important Job in the Big City, then getting your own business established. A few "special days" each year weren't enough to make up for missed family dinners, baseball games, school plays. You weren't around to tuck me in and read me stories.

I shut you out more and more as I got older, resenting your absence, and the missed opportunity to feel like Daddy's little girl. By my teenage years, we could barely speak to each other. Years passed but nothing changed, and when I got married, I walked alone down the aisle.

The year that my marriage failed, you gave me *The Runaway Bunny* for Christmas. Your inscription told me that I was *your* runaway bunny, and that you would always be there if I needed you. I kept a stony face, but I cried as I drove home, wishing I could believe what you had said.

Because when I remembered the story from my childhood, it was my mother's voice that I heard.

BRONTË
Wuthering Heights

My mother's battered copy of *Wuthering Heights,* a thick book left on a dusty table in our basement, had yellowing pages and tiny type, wrinkled edges and highlighted passages. My mother came from China, an ambitious young woman who believed life in Canada would be better. Upon her acceptance to university, she was required to go through a reading list of English books. *Wuthering Heights* was one of them, and she purchased an English-Chinese edition at her local bookstore.

Its curious cover captured my attention from the first time I set eyes on it as a child. A photo of a young girl and a boy whose face was covered in grime and dirt. They sat together on straw mats, the boy leaning over the girl's shoulder as she read a book. I would fall in love with that boy, the girl, and their twisted but beautiful story.

My mother understood the importance of reading, and so from an early age she read me book after book, filling me with story upon story every day after work. Sometimes she would be so tired that she would read to me from the sofa, her work clothes still on. But she still read, and that was the beginning of my love of books.

I was ten when I first read it. This was not one of the books my mother encouraged me to read. She didn't like seeing me with it, which only increased my curiosity. Looking back, I still wonder how the ten-year-old me would have been into a classic like that. At first I read the novel only because I wasn't supposed to. And then my intentions were true and pure, and they grew to embrace and love the story like it was a part of me.

It remains, to this day, my favourite book. I have argued with myself countless times on what my second, third, and fourth favourite books are. I constantly change the rank of the books I read as I enjoy one more than the other. But, hands down, *Wuthering Heights* will always hold a sincere and secure place in my heart.

It taught me, in many ways, how beauty and ugliness are not equal reflections of the other. It taught me how love could be twisted, overwhelming, and all consuming. It taught me that fires within people could burn for an eternity, through death and beyond. It started my belief in ghosts, my paranoia of the dark, a thirst for all the right words, and my ideas of soul mates.

It has shaped me, without a doubt. I loved the story; I loved the characters; I loved the book for what it was and what it made me. And for this book, with all its breathtaking imagery and heart-twisting ambitions, I will be forever grateful.

SETH
A Suitable Boy

He gave me this book a year and a half ago, for our one-year anniversary. He said he saw it in the bookstore and thought of me. I didn't know whether to be confused or even slightly offended, or to laugh. Since both our families are of Indian descent, we both knew what the words "a suitable boy" really meant. I asked him if he'd read it and he said yes and joked about its length (about fourteen hundred pages). I was in college at the time and barely had time to breathe much less read a fourteen-hundred-page, not-required-for-class novel, so I put it on my bedside table and left it there for about two months, though I wouldn't say I'd forgotten about it. I finally started reading the book during spring break. I don't even remember packing it. Since my old-fashioned, totally traditional parents did not approve of me dating, I had to hide the fact that I was meeting a guy at the airport along with my girl friends. I finally started reading it on the plane, with him sitting right next to me, sleeping peacefully for most of the six-hour flight.

Once I started the book, I couldn't put it down. Within the first fifty pages I understood why he loved the book and why he'd given it to me. The book's main protagonist is a girl who, in the simplest form, is trying to find herself and make her own decisions and choices. Parts of the book reminded me of myself. Some conversations between Lata (the main character) and her mother were similar to those I'd had with my parents. By the time we landed in Mexico I'd read nearly a third of it. He smiled when he saw how far I'd gotten and, kissing me, said that he knew I'd love it. I spent the first two days in Mexico sunbathing and reading. A couple of my friends were irritated at me for reading so much; others understood. He, well, he just laughed every time someone tried to take the book from me and I protested. I was in my room on our second night when I finished reading. It was about seven p.m., and everyone was getting ready to head to dinner and then to the clubs.

On the very last page of the book he'd written, "After reading about the search for suitable boys, I hope you know that I want to be the suitable boy for you. I love you." Tears came to my eyes as I read the last line. It was the first time he'd told me he loved me since we'd decided early on in our relationship to not say the word "love" until we truly meant it. I grabbed the book and ran to his room next door and banged on the door. The instant he opened it, I launched myself into his arms and told him I loved him, too.

Now, a year and a half after he gave the book to me, I'm preparing for my wedding. My family found the "suitable boy" for me and I can't wait to marry him. I've known he was the "suitable boy" for me for more than a year now.

MAYHEW
The Soup Bible

We were only supposed to be having fun. A fling. We weren't supposed to be getting to know each other or doing sweet things for one another or even really caring about the other, if I'm going to be perfectly frank. We did talk about books, though. We shared some of the same favorites: Hemingway, Fitzgerald, Huxley. But this story isn't about one of those books. One day I made an off-hand comment and mentioned that I loved making soup on cold winter weekends, that it reminded me of home. That it gave me comfort. A week later he left this on the seat of my car, said it had made him think of me when he saw it. Said he hoped that someday I would cook him something from it. It was the first gift he ever gave me. And without realizing it, that was the moment I let my guard down; the moment I thought that, maybe, this was something more than fun. Over the next several weeks, we fell in love, and though we have exchanged many books since, this one will always be the most precious.

SUSKIND
Perfume

It was brief, one night only, really, followed by years of correspondence which continues to this day. It wasn't meant to be: he was a decade and a half older, living in a different state in a long-term relationship. I was young, but he was infatuated and he sent me this book, his favourite, to read on a holiday with another man. The holiday never happened, but my relationship with the other man did and continues to this day. Still, this book is now my favourite and I love the mind of the man who gave it to me.

GHOSH
The Calcutta Chromosome

This was the last book he gave me. I was in hospital, recovering from a tropical illness. He sat uneasily in the visitor's chair. Contagious microorganisms and the possibility of meeting my family or friends caused him some discomfort. Still, he'd come. He brought me three books from his bedside pile: *The Tales of Hoffman,* Gerard de Nerval's *Selected Writings,* and this book by Amitav Ghosh. More precious to me because they came from the pile under his bed.

Most of his books in my bookshelf are from his academic library. When we first met he was my language teacher: a heady combination of a Latin accent and green cat's eyes flecked with amber. He is married (so was I at that stage); neither of us was young anymore. We both were interested in mysticism, history, conspiracy theories, and sex.

The novel uses actual research behind the transmission of the malaria parasite; to follow a fictional, Indian scientific/mystical cult, exploring the possibility of chromosomal genetic transfers. Not an easy read, it is nevertheless fascinating.

He said good-bye again yesterday. In four years he has said this many times, and always in February. This last book requires more than one reading. Its conclusion is unresolved and unsatisfying, much like us.

PLASCENCIA
The People of Paper

I am a book collector and writer. I tend to gravitate toward modern works and usually collect first editions of books that mean a great deal to me. When I met my boyfriend one of the first things we ever talked about was books. We share an immense passion for reading and writing. During that first conversation, one of the books I discussed was one of my absolute favorites and was read as part of a list of required texts in an honors lit class in undergrad.

Later, after we started dating, I gave him my copy to read. He was just as amazed by it as I was. Not only is the writing moving, and even strange at times, it's the almost graphic characteristics the author uses that bring the pages to life. The author cut out certain words, blacked out entire paragraphs, and actually restarts the story from the beginning in the middle of the book. It's certainly not a traditional read, and is one of the most innovative books I've ever seen.

A couple of years ago, for Christmas, I unwrapped a first edition of this book and I was astounded. The fact that my boyfriend understood how the book shaped me, how I see the world, changed my idea of writing, and that it was a collectible was so perfect.

Five years later, I see the book and I still smile. It is one of the best gifts I've ever gotten.

NABOKOV
The Original of Laura

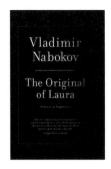

On our second date, my boyfriend gave me a book that I already own. It was sweet and thoughtful, until I learned he had actually regifted it to me.

It's okay. I still love you.

CREELEY
For Love: Poems 1950–1960

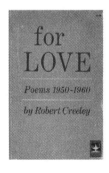

It was a beat-up used hardcover. Gifted with a dead rose and a fresh unsigned poem tucked into it, which extolled the virtues of thigh irises and coarse hands. Wrapped in a Crown Heights Chinese takeout menu with red crayon hearts. Very classic. Very sexy. And the giver and the gift both still inhabit my tiny studio apartment today, so apparently it was a good gift.

LEVITHAN
The Lover's Dictionary

It's not mine, though I've no intention of returning it anytime soon. We'd been pen pals for months when you sent it to me, and it was overshadowed by the wonderful birthday present included in the package. I didn't get around to reading it for a while, and when I did finally pick it up, I was high on Vicodin, thanks to the wonders of wisdom teeth removal and terrible dry socket. The first words were like a sucker punch to the heart. Months of hiding, telling myself I didn't adore you, wasn't falling for a boy hundreds of miles away, vanished. I grabbed a handful of sticky notes—I had the good sense not to write in a book that wasn't mine—and marked page after page, plastering my high, tired, emotionally drained self across the margins in a spine of color-coordinated tabs.

I was better organized high than I ever was sober.

Not long after, you asked me out—inasmuch as anyone can be asked out when there are states between them—and I said yes. Now, months later, *The Lover's Dictionary* still sits on my windowsill, each tab still in place. It feels just as true now as it did back then, but now I smile every time I pick it up. I still have no plans to give it back.

CERVANTES
Don Quixote

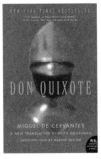

He handed me a rectangular package, carefully wrapped in plain brown paper. He watched with anticipation as I gingerly opened it to reveal a large hardcover book with a glossy crimson slipcover. He worked in a bookshop. Perhaps subconsciously, I took this as an indication that we would connect on a much deeper level than I had with my ex-boyfriend.

On our second date, he sported a messenger bag with a copy of *The Catcher in the Rye* prominently sticking out of one of the side pockets. At dinner, I could no longer contain my excitement and asked him about his favorite part of the book.

He sheepishly admitted he had never read the book, but carried it around "to look cool." My jaw dropped in astonishment. On further pressing, he revealed that he didn't really read books. Or magazines. Or newspapers.

At that moment I should have gotten up from the table in that Korean restaurant and walked out, as surely as I would have had he kicked a puppy or elbowed an elderly person in the face. I didn't, though, and that relationship limped on for a few years before it completely fizzled out (to our great mutual relief).

After the breakup, I was disillusioned, yes. I had put more faith in him than he deserved, but this somehow didn't tarnish my hope that there were good men out there—worthy men.

As I hugged the crimson tome to my chest, I realized my faith had been rewarded. Most of the time, windmills are just windmills, no matter how hard you try to imagine them otherwise. Sometimes, though, the dreamers in this world are gifted with a special kind of magic—as long as they keep looking for it.

The Oxford English Dictionary

I'd planned to give him this as a wedding gift. It was perfect for a man like him.

Turned out he already had it, and we were never anywhere as close to getting married as I thought we were. I think I misread him.

MROŻEK
The Elephant

I married my wife on December 17. We had been so busy getting ourselves ready for the big day that Christmas was no more than an afterthought. I knew what to get her, but she was rather in a panic about what I might like, and she asked me what she should get. I can always do with more books, even though we have so many in our rented apartment here in Poland that the shelves are overflowing.

I had read with amazement and pure jealousy of a woman who decided to buy over $10,000 worth of Penguin Classics from Amazon. I love the gray spines of the Puffin Modern Classics, the black spines with red text that Penguin also publishes, and I like *The New York Review of Books* series. I have a stack of old orange-spined Penguins, but here they're not easy to come by.

I sent my wife off whilst I enjoyed a coffee and another couple of chapters of the Chinua Achebe book I was reading. When she returned an hour later, she told me she'd bought not one but three books by Polish literati. I was thrilled. The book that caught my eye was, again, a Penguin: *The Elephant* by Sławomir Mrożek.

I made sure to finish the Achebe so that on Christmas Day I could begin *The Elephant* immediately, and I'm now ever so thankful that my wife has such good taste. *The Elephant* is an incredible book, a collection of forty-two short stories that span only 160-odd pages, but they are all masterpieces. One of the most treasured memories I have from my teenage years is discovering Kafka and struggling through *The Castle*. Mrożek comes from the same tradition, highlighting with his expert eye the hypocrisy and sadness of totalitarianism.

I hope soon to buy an apartment for my wife and me to start a family in; when I do, I know which book will take pride of place.

KENYON
The Writer's Digest Character Naming Sourcebook

It was a reference book, the sort of book you pick up when you need it, but rarely spend much time with because it soon becomes boring and repetitive. An apt metaphor for our relationship, which began and ended many times over the course of six years before we finally got engaged in 2009. That lasted seventeen months.

This is the only book she ever gave me and, though I kept it after we broke up, she returned all the ones I had given her. "For my namer of things," she wrote inside, hoping that I would use it to create richer characters. She was the closed parenthesis to my open parenthesis, but even with the help of this book I was unable to name her properly, until it was too late.

I tried to call her my wife, but she was just my friend.

Redacted

I can't. I can't show you the cover, and I can't give you her name.

We met at a friend's cocktail party, and while she was luscious and magnetic and I wanted to spend all my time buried in her, locked in her messy studio apartment in Brooklyn, talking endlessly about nothing, watching TV naked, making toast and scrambled eggs and going back to bed, it didn't last. We were together for just a couple of months.

She gave me a copy of her book, which she'd uploaded to a print-on-demand service because, she said, she didn't have the patience to wait for her big break to happen. There is a beauty in the fact that she didn't really seem to care whether she was "really" published, and that she didn't seem to care how awful her writing was. I tried to read the book, but I just couldn't. I loved her, a little, and I loved her exuberance and warmth and utter self-possession. But I didn't love her enough.

RAND
Atlas Shrugged

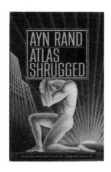

He gave this book to me two months after he moved in, when we were just roommates and nothing more. He said it was his favorite, so I should read it and write notes in the margins. So I did. I read it, and he read it to me, and I underlined beautiful phrases and fell into a sort of love. I was two hundred pages from the end when we broke.

When he moved out, he asked to take it with him. I had grown to hate the book and was never going to finish it, and it was still his favorite. I gave it back to him, gladly. It still has my words and scribbles inside; he'll never understand what any of them mean.

PYNCHON
Gravity's Rainbow

I had an affair with a girl at work. We built our relationship on quixotic, pie-in-the-sky ideals. Reality offered harsh reconciliation. We came from different worlds, and it wouldn't last outside our bubble.

The relationship ended for a while and started back up again. During our time apart, she created a list of books that I loved, that she wanted to read, most notably *Gravity's Rainbow*. She told me this was the book she wanted to read the most. She said if she finished it, and made sense of it, we were meant to be.

I gave her my copy, engulfed with marginalia. Our relationship ended—for good this time—before she made much progress in it. My copy is still with her, I think. And I doubt she'll finish it. "Fuck the war. They're in love."

PULLMAN
His Dark Materials: The Golden Compass, The Subtle Knife, The Amber Spyglass

Our first (and only) Christmas together was shortly after we started dating. It's always awkward buying for such a big holiday in a new relationship, and knowing I'm difficult to buy for anyway, I told him to get me *His Dark Materials*. I desperately wanted a specific version, and I described not only the covers of the books but also the exact location of them in the store. Christmas Day, I didn't get the versions I wanted, but the paperback combo pack. I still appreciated them, but later found out he had never even looked for the books himself. He had stood at the customer service desk while someone else fetched the books for him. I should have known at that moment it wasn't going to work.

A few weeks later we got into a fight and one of the things he was mad about was that I hadn't even looked at the books since he'd given them to me. I tried to explain that choosing a book to read is an art. There's a magic to it, and when you read the right book at the right time it becomes so much more than just a book; it becomes a symbol for that moment. He scoffed at the notion. Not long after, I did begin reading the series and, boy, was I right about picking the right moment. I was about halfway through *The Subtle Knife* when I was completely and utterly inspired by the series through a reading of Plato's *Republic* we had just done in my philosophy class. I emailed my professor and begged her to let me write my first paper on Pullman and Plato, which she encouraged me to do. As the due date for the paper closed in, I still had a lot of reading left to finish, so I opted to stay home on a Saturday night with a bottle of wine, my book, and the house all to myself. That didn't go over well and another blowout between us ensued. I couldn't understand what he wanted from me, and he couldn't understand why I would want to sit at home by myself on a Saturday night. Everyone around me told me to give in, to stay in on Sunday and read then, but I'm stubborn and impossible and refused. I think that was the moment it all ended for me.

We lasted a while longer, but in my heart I knew it wasn't right. He cried when I let him go and told me he loved me and would give me everything and anything I wanted if only I would stay. I knew better than to believe a man who cringed at the idea of setting foot in a bookstore and wouldn't even deign to get the books off the shelves himself. He could never have given me what I wanted, but his books did get me an A+ on my philosophy paper, and for that I'll always be grateful.

EUGENIDES
Middlesex

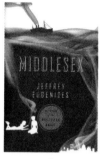

Those old Greeks knew how to get it done. Maybe Callie Stephanides would agree. There are characters that start out on paper, and then you read them and somehow they slip from the binds of the book, and before you know it they've acquired a spirit that floats around your head, saying the things you know they would and smirking slyly at all the goings-on.

I was on the outs when Callie started haunting me, hovering unobtrusively like this bit of flotsam on the top of my mind, so I had to go through her to think at all. I was broke, wandering the city with my friend J., reeling from unexpected death and knowing tragedy, trying to get a handle on the world, on maybe . . . who I was.

And Callie . . . we were sitting on the porch and J. handed it to me. This perfectly sized book, a dark smoky cover with silhouettes and a ship at sea. *Middlesex.*

The book ate me up. It swallowed me whole and in its belly I found Callie. Set out from her family's heritage and eventually here we both were in her adolescence, in the middle of storm and fire. Sentences did not sit on the paper; they melted and formed themselves onto some secret section of my heart. If a book has never saved your life, you might not understand that they are not just tomes for stories, but that they can heal, can bring you back from the edge, can give you sanity. Callie was a kind spirit when I was lost, sad beyond mortal ken, yearning for something I could not name. The book was warm, soft, glittering, and wise. I sailed with it to Byzantine.

PAUSCH & ZASLOW
The Last Lecture

All but one of the books were stolen. I took them at the dissolution of each connection; unwilling keepsakes of soured attempts at love. Unable to make off with their hearts, I instead secreted away their favourite stories. From him, I took Mitch Albom. From her, Meir Shalev. From him, Greg Bear, and on it went. A single novel from each failed relationship, or almost-relationship, gathering dust in a growing collection I kept well apart from the other books.

With this one, I made the mistake of disclosing my shameful habit. He teased it out of me between his black sheets gridded with white lines. I expected a rebuke, but he merely laughed, offering some quip about how his bookshelf was at capacity anyhow. It was . . . and that was one of the things I liked best about him. Psychology, computer science, world affairs, and science fiction were packed together, neatly stacked both vertically and horizontally, slotted into every available inch. All at once over and under one another, holding each other fast in place. They were like our conversations, which strayed between science, gossip, and

philosophy but were always impressed into a modicum of unification by our mutual love of logic.

Each time I ventured into his bachelor pad I sat on the windowsill next to the young Norfolk Island pine. With one hand resting in its latticework of needles, the other would stray to the bookshelf. My fingers selected some new gem that I had not noticed . . . Nietzsche, Asimov, Kierkegaard, Dawkins. I would extract it gently and ask him where it came from before tetris-ing it securely back into place. As I replaced it, he would look up from furiously typing white code on black screens. His words were always the same.

"Have you read it? No? You must . . . it will change your life."

I never read them, and I blame him for that. He gave no indication of priority. I could not tell which, if any, held particular personal significance . . . perhaps they all were equally transformative. When the time came to steal one, I had no idea what book to take. He was in the shower, washing away the last vestiges of my scent off his skin. I was bleary-eyed, desperate, helpless in the face of the crammed bookshelf. I had to steal something of great value, but nothing stood out from the tight and even grid of spines. I heard the water shut off. I backed away, empty-handed, knocking the pine from the sill in my haste. I was cleaning the soil from the floor when he emerged and told me it was time to go.

I had known our narrative was ending long before it did. He was moving across the ocean in the new year, and we never planned for an epic tale. What I did not expect was for him to cut things off abruptly, weeks early, after an ill-timed phone call rattled his calm. I ran out of time to watch his oft-detached gaze stir with excitement when he explained complex mathematical theories in words I could almost understand. I ran out of time to determine which story possessed the power to stir his rational heart. Before I could steal from him, he was gone.

At the end of that frigid December, he called me unexpectedly and asked me to meet him for lunch. He felt bad about the way things had passed. With the plotline severed prematurely, our narrative ached for conclusion. Across an unfinished wood table we made small talk about neuroscience before moving into more tender territory. He told me that the pine was in his car. Of the people close to him, he knew I would take care of it best.

He then slid a package across to my clasped hands, gesturing for me to open it. Neatly wrapped in brown paper was *The Last Lecture* by Randy Pausch. Between sips of black coffee, he told me, "It is a simple book containing a dying professor's last lecture. Dr. Pausch is a professor in my field, human-computer interactions. He may be a geek but he is one I can identify with and one who has learned to inspire. He hasn't died yet, but he is about to."

He went on, "I think we can all do worse than follow a little of his structure. I think this book is a fitting gift, given what we talk about and how our minds work. I would be pleased to find you agree."

When I arrived home, I added Pausch to my own bookshelf, forcing a gift to earn its place amongst stolen treasure. I stepped back and widened my gaze, taking a little time to admire the collection of novels pilfered from the women and men I had given my own trusted stories. A couple of years later, he asked me what happened to the pine. I didn't tell him I had buried it in the forest—that during our final meeting as lovers, it had frozen to death in the car.

PANCAKE
The Stories of Breece D'J Pancake

She found it in the remainder aisle at our local bookstore. She had read Breece D'J Pancake's collection of shorts during college and wanted me to share in his prose. I knew this was the end of us. We cried knowing this was the last time I'd get to hold her in my arms. The weight of being with me was more than she could take. She headed back to her home to marry the man her family approved of. I've read these little gems of short stories again and again. It feels fitting that she gave me his only published collection. Our brief relationship was like that book: glorious. I still cherish my copy with the wine stain, at peace with the fact that somewhere out there she's thinking about this book as well.

OCHSNER
People I Wanted To Be

It was a ghostly book he gave me, and it haunted me even after the smell of his hair had left my pillow and the letter he sent asking for his book back had been thoroughly buried by new mail. I hope he understood, even when writing that letter, that I wouldn't reply—this cursed relationship we had conformed to its own sort of justice, and the realization of our betrayal afterward was its price.

We lived for a while in a bubble, ignoring the fact that only weeks before his seemingly perfect relationship with my best friend had crumbled, as had my friendship with her. We idled in restaurants and gently poked fun at her more eccentric qualities in a ritual both awkward and cleansing. He taught me to tango the night I sneaked him into my room; I skipped orchestra to go to his house, to lie in his bed and pick through his cigar box of memories of her. This book was among a few he gave to me, and I devoured it overnight, but the book itself was peripheral to the image I wanted to have of him; in each story I read I hungered for an affirmation of "us."

From the start we were doomed completely to be haunted by this absent girl, and we were equally captivated by the ethereal illicitness of what might have been and the bruising, inexorable weight of the truth—that anything we could have would be unavoidably tainted by the heartache that had happened to bring us together. This book still sits on my bookshelf, and I am unable to bring myself to put it in storage. It lurks in the corner, as does the memory of him. Sometimes, late at night, I slide it from its spot on my bookcase and look at the cover for a few minutes. One day, I will choose either to read the book and remember or to give it away and attempt to forget him.

NERUDA
Twenty Love Poems and a Song of Despair

How about a book I wished he gave me?

I think I fell in love with him when he mentioned Neruda on our first date. I was amazed that he recited some of the poems from memory. We were inseparable from then on. Sometimes, he'd sit next to me at work, and one day he shared with me a PDF file of Neruda's poems. He read to me "Your Feet" and declared it as mine, his "little tower." Nobody had dedicated a poem to me before.

The first few months were amazing, a haze of love. And then one day he just got out of that haze and stopped loving me. I tried desperately to please him, to make him call me Little Tower again.

He went to his hometown for the weekend and visited his father. When he got back, he told me that he had planned to bring me a Neruda book from his personal library, but he didn't. "Oh, why didn't you? I would have liked that." He said he didn't know why he decided not to. Instead, he brought with him three books. The only one I can recall was erotic literature. He said he brought them to use as material for his job.

I knew then that he didn't care for me anymore, and that's when I started to give up.

And Neruda is my favorite no longer.

McCOURT
Angela's Ashes

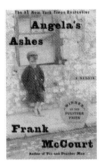

He made me fall back in love with words. After giving me Vonnegut, Heller, Salinger, and Orwell, my first love shyly offered his copy of *Angela's Ashes* to me. He said, "You must read it and maybe it will make your own problems feel a little less bad."

Soon we became just like strangers again and I curiously picked it off my bookshelf and immersed myself in the story he loved so much, grasping for anything that would let me feel him again. Now it's been a year since I spoke to him last, and even longer since we were close, but it's still the book I turn to when I need to feel like home.

ARTHUR
The Autumn People

When I was a child, my parents, brothers, and I spent our summers travelling through France by car, our destination being four weeks at a small Spanish resort by the sea, a veritable paradise. I whiled away the long hours in the back of the car with a box of books; without it that would have been a very long journey indeed. As I got older, I became an increasingly voracious reader and I realised, while packing my books for the summer when I was eight, that I had read all the books I then owned. It being unthinkable to travel without books, I decided to pack my favourites, but Mum and Dad bought me one new book—Ruth Arthur's *The Autumn People*. I have never forgotten it.

The Autumn People tells two intertwined stories. During a summer holiday on the Scottish island of Karasay, the contemporary heroine Romilly Williams falls under the spell cast upon her great-grandmother by a man whose ghost now haunts her. I loved the story and the setting. Most important, it introduced me to the artist, designer, and writer William Morris, as Romilly is a budding artist whose own art is compared to Morris's designs. I was unable to find out more about him or to see any of his designs until we returned home where I could get to the library, but I did spend the summer drawing my own botanical designs from nature, fabric, and every other available source of inspiration.

I have managed to get rid of only a small number of books in my life, so as my personal library grew, *The Autumn People* and other books were put into boxes in the attic. When I went back to find my copy of the book, the box in which it was packed had disappeared. I sometimes like to entertain the suspicion that the ghost in the story made off with it. While the book may now be long lost, my love of William Morris and his work has endured. I finally decided to buy another copy, and now own a simply decorated hardback edition, and I still draw my own patterns inspired by William Morris.

KLOSTERMAN
Killing Yourself to Live: 85% of a True Story

He gave me this book after the first time we slept together. I was heading back home on a plane that day, across a great distance that I thought we could bridge. It was funny and poignant. I still love the book, having spent an entire plane ride highlighting passages, fragments of a love I think he meant for me to uncover and use to decipher his intentions.

KEROUAC
The Subterraneans

When we met I was entirely too young. He was so beautiful it nearly hurt to look at him too long. He was a decade older. I was young, wild, and trying entirely too hard to act tough. He seemed to understand that I was already wounded. He left me with a copy of Kerouac's *The Subterraneans*. Inside the front cover he inscribed, "To Pocahontas, living in a clusterfuck."

Our love was short. I still wonder what he meant to say.

JOYCE
Ulysses

We were going to read it together, page by page, and unravel it as we went. Together. And even though we would be at different schools, we would stay together, bound together by this book and the medium of words, of email and phone calls.

We got as far as Buck Mulligan's crusty razor.

That's what young love is supposed to be like, I'm told. And I still haven't read *Ulysses*.

KRAKAUER
Into the Wild

She was a sweet girl, all open and honest, no trace of pretense, of calculation. In her daffodil yellow dress, her deep tan, all curls and boobs and big bug-eyed sunglasses. Nothing at all like the tough girls I imagined myself with, the pale vampires with their tattoos and pixie cuts and slim boyish hips.

I won her affection with a cough drop. I made her a mix CD of indie rock and postpunk. The songs said nothing about me, about how I felt or was capable of feeling, about what she meant to me (perhaps, in the end a godsend, this). It read like a tutorial on what a girlfriend of mine should be listening to. God, what an asshole I was.

She gave me this. A book she loved and wanted me to have because of how important it was to her. A book I read and loathed for being so straightforward, so heart-on-sleeve. A book with a few obvious lessons, joys, and admonitions I was too cynical to take to heart or even hand.

Yeah, it was a selfish short-lived relationship. I was never in love but enjoyed the attention of someone who clearly was. How shitty is that? No, don't answer.

QUINN
Ishmael: An Adventure of the Mind and Spirit

Years earlier I had been in his short film based on this book. I didn't know the book and didn't really know him and I still don't know why he asked me, a writer, to play the only character in the film, when we went to a school filled with actresses. I don't take direction well and had to lie on a cat-hair-strewn floor a lot, which wasn't fun. Later we spent a couple hours in a sound-proof room to record the voiceover, which could have been fun because I thought he was really good-looking, but it wasn't because (see above) I don't take direction well.

We stayed in touch, and eventually he moved to New York and in with some mutual friends of ours. Also, eventually, his new girl-friend, an actual actress, rerecorded the voiceover, but I don't like to think about that.

We started hanging out one-on-one when he moved out of that apartment, and we didn't have the chance to run into each other conveniently as much. We exchanged many books. Neither of us ever thought of it as a prelude to a romance, we just liked hanging out, and books, and theater and talking and drinking and things. He gave me *Ishmael* to read over Christmas two years ago. I read it in a single gulp on Christmas Day. I hated the book but liked reading it, and thinking about the conversation we would have about it, and all my valid reasons for hating it and being directed.

When we got back to the city we went to dinner, and then to a play, and then to a bar and another bar and closed that bar out and stayed there arguing until dawn. We consider that night our anniversary. Now we live together and *Ishmael* is on a shelf of his books, underneath a shelf of my books. I still hate the book, and I still love giving him books and reading books he gives me.

BRADBURY
Fahrenheit 451

I was eleven and reading everything in sight. My dad gave me Vonnegut and my mom gave me Alcott. But he gave me Bradbury.

I wanted to read this one at my tiny Catholic school, but I was only in sixth grade, and it was in the restricted seventh and eighth grade mature content section. The irony didn't strike me until much, much later that they were denying me a book about censorship and book burning, but when I came home and told him he was livid. I was happy to have someone on my side and never expected anything to come of it.

The school never caved, but a month later, at Christmas, there was a book under the tree, wrapped and addressed to me. In later years he would give me my first beautiful and coveted edition of the full works of Shakespeare and the beat poets, *The Feminine Mystique,* and the memoirs that would start me writing. But that Christmas, with Bradbury, he handed me the book they said I shouldn't read and started my journey with a few words of his own, "Little

Sister: Read everything you can. Learn about all the ideas that this world has to offer. Subvert Authority! Love always, your big brother."

McKILLIP
Riddle-Master

Even as a young child I loved to read. I used to sit down and disappear into the world of the latest book I was reading for hours and hours. I gave away many books that I loved to friends, lovers, and family, if I thought they'd like them. When my younger brother got old enough to read I started passing on some of my books to him. When he reached middle school, he stopped reading and said he hated it. I kept on passing  along books I thought he'd enjoy and eventually, before his sophomore year in high school, he started reading again.

I moved to the other side of the country to go to graduate school last year. When I got to my new city, I opened my suitcase and inside was *Riddle-Master*. He'd written inside the front jacket that I'd always given him books he'd loved and that showed him how much I love him. He said he wanted to give me a book that he loved and enjoyed and hoped I would, too. He also said that he hoped this book would remind me that I can read for pleasure, too, while I'm drowning in graduate school reading.

Riddle-Master is one of my all-time favorite books. Not only because it's a great book and trilogy, but because it was the first book my little brother gave me.

BRYSON
The Mother Tongue—English and How It Got That Way

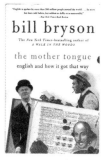

It was a Christmas present. One book among many, most of which I'd already read; my mom was lucky if she could find a book I hadn't already devoured. But this one was different. I loved the way it sat in my hands, weighty in a paperback's gentle way, and I loved the promise of the nonfiction, despite the heavy reality of facts. I was fifteen and didn't care much for them.

My mother knew—knows—me far better than I gave her credit for. I inhaled the story—and it was a story, well and brilliantly told—and I was hooked. I'd always had a deep, passionate love for words, but ambitions of becoming a writer or an editor didn't seem quite right. Bryson introduced me to the idea of linguistics as a study, and the next several months of bookstore visits found me in the language section, reading—and buying—everything I could get my hands on.

Now, four years later, I am a freshman in college, majoring in linguistics and loving every minute of it. I could only take a handful of books with me to university, most of which are well-worn fiction favourites, but Bryson sits in the place of honour on the windowsill beside me, loved and dog-eared, and with my mom's inscription on the inside cover. I have to wonder if she knew, when she bought it, what she was getting me into.

DICKENS
Great Expectations

This was a going-to-college present, marking one of the most significant transitions of my life, which included leaving my family and my country and immersing myself in a completely foreign country, language, and culture.

He is everything a man should be: confident, intelligent, entrepreneurial, courageous, adventurous, wise, handsome . . . the list can go on forever. He is one of the few men in my life whom I truly look up to, respect, and admire. He was my English tutor, my mentor, my role model.

He is responsible for half of my English vocabulary, and if I could ever call myself a writer of any eloquence, I would owe it to him. His patient guidance and teaching throughout my high school career have given me knowledge beyond words and their literal meaning, but the ideas and strength they carry. He has shown me that, with ambition and passion, anything is possible and I am capable of anything. That, his belief in my potential, is the greatest gift and the greatest expectation.

DU BOIS
W.E.B. Du Bois: A Reader

I was a working-class girl with only a high school diploma; he had a degree in philosophy from a private university. I sometimes would have to go home and look up words he used when we were together. His intelligence was a turn on, as was his kind heart. We fell in love and moved in together. When one more dead-end job left me disappointed, I decided to start taking classes at the community college up the street. I was completely intimidated by the thought of going to college. It was all a mystery to me and I felt I didn't deserve to be there. He talked me through it, explained everything, demystified the process, and promised me that I belonged there. When it came time to register for classes my first semester he held my hand through the registration line. I don't think I would have made it through without him.

I did well in my classes and found myself drawn to the social sciences. I was completely taken by the works of W.E.B. Du Bois. For my birthday my second year in college, he gave me a copy of *W.E.B. Du Bois, A Reader*. On the inside cover my lover wrote: "Happy Birthday, My Woman! Rejoice in your heroes!" After finishing community college I transferred to a four-year college. By the time I finished my bachelor's degree, our love had withered and died. Shortly after, I moved far away to attend graduate school. Now, all these years later, I am a full-time university professor teaching in the social sciences. W.E.B. Du Bois remains one of my heroes. So, too, does that young man who held my hand through the registration line, who kept telling me that I belonged there—even when I couldn't imagine it.

MARTEL
Life of Pi

I knew what it was as soon as he gave me the package in the airport. He was never good with surprises. I didn't read the book until I was safe in the confines of my room in the States; throughout the twelve-hour journey home, I never made it past the note he wrote on the cover. I missed him too much.

I wanted to love it as much as he did. But I couldn't.

He didn't like the book I gave him half as much as I love it. It might be a sign that our time together was not meant to go beyond that summer, no matter how much we wanted it to.

COHEN
Leonard Cohen

He was mystery itself. In a tweed sports coat with patched elbows, he'd stride into the bookstore-café in which I worked and come up to my counter. He was beyond handsome: blondish, with deep green eyes and an ever-present smile. He'd talk with my manager, a friend of his, shoot me one more devastating glance, then disappear. I asked the manager, "Who is he?" N. would give me a serious look and say, "Don't get involved with him. You don't want to know him." This intrigued me all the more. Weeks later, he'd show up again, all charming smiles and impeccable manners. I'm not sure how he managed to project such a powerful aura of enticing danger, considering that he looked like a literature professor, but he did. He'd ask me what sort of books I liked, and finally, the last time I ever saw him, he told me I should listen to Leonard Cohen, that I'd love him.

I never even found out his name. He might have been the ghost of books to be read or a shadow of a man I'd later meet and fall in love with who looks just like him. But it's possible that the mutability of memory has given them the same face.

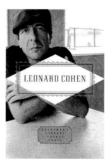

Both men used books to get to me, to get into the heart of me.

And I never listened to Leonard Cohen, nor read his poems. Until yesterday. I bought this, and I consider it a gift from a ghost, from memory, from my past. Maybe he was some dark, bookish angel, sent to seduce me around the right way, to realize what I should have been doing. He failed, and it took me a dozen more years to figure these things out for myself.

ISHIGURO
Never Let Me Go

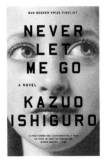

We'd met on a summer human rights fellowship in Paris. She had a boyfriend; I couldn't keep my mind off her. When we returned to the States— she began law school in New York, I stayed with family in Boston—we thought it was over. But I convinced her to let me visit her for one week-end in August. I took the Fung Wah Chinatown bus to Canal Street, where she picked me up. We rode the subway giddily, tongue-tied, and vaguely aware of the surrealism of lasting past our expiry date.

We left her room once all weekend to pick up some fast food. When she dropped me off at Canal Street the next day, she was wearing a white blouse and handed me a book: *Never Let Me Go* by Kazuo Ishiguro. I wouldn't see her again for two months, a gap that seemed to stretch to eternity at the time. But that book—and her inscription inside, thanking me for visiting her—sustained me until our next meeting.

It's been over three years now. I'm back in Paris doing a master's program; she's in Alaska clerking for a judge. Sometimes I open my mailbox to find a new shipment of books; sometimes she opens hers to discover the same. She still has a boyfriend, but this time it's me.

MAUGHAM
Of Human Bondage

He gave it to me on my birthday, with a grin on his face. It was his favorite book and he wanted me to read it. We had just begun what I consider to be one of the most intimate phases of a relationship: the phase where you start sharing the books you love.

I read it and loved it. But it became very clear to me that this was a book that spoke to him more than it could ever speak to me. He thought he was Philip Carey. He thought that he had suffered through relationships with women who were like Mildred in the story. It spoke to him because he had been imprisoned by unrequited love in the past. As the relationship devolved, I kept coming back to this book in my head. As he belittled me and drove me to things that I never thought I would do for another human being, I realized that he had related to this book in a completely incorrect way. He was not the foolish Carey, doing anything and everything to win the love of Mildred. Instead, I was the one who had taken on the Carey role. Cleaning his house for parties I wasn't invited to, spending money I didn't have on gifts to win his affection. And he was Mildred, cruel to the last. I can only be grateful that I didn't suffer financial ruin at the hand of him, although I suppose I came close.

I only hope that one day I can meet my Sally and get on with my life.

LIGHTMAN
Einstein's Dreams

We spent a long weekend together, after meeting through a group of mutual friends. We had an immediate, simple chemistry that trumped how little we had in common. The lack of conversation could have been uncomfortable if it hadn't been so unbelievably clear to me that this was the most pleasant kind of temporary: a stopgap on the way to other people, places, things. He was reading this pint-size book for one of his classes. As he read, he underlined a passage and said it had reminded him of me. He read it out loud, shifting his eyes up to find mine and parse my response.

I took the book and devoured the petite read that same afternoon. The alternate theories of time and the dreamlike quality to each vignette were romantic. I almost confused my love for the book with feelings for this relative stranger. Almost. The weekend ended and he gave me the book to keep. It remains on my bookshelf ten years later, underlined in his hand and mine, read and reread.

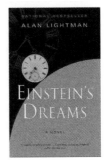

KRAUSS
The Physics of Star Trek

The first thing he ever gave me was a book; we'd only started dating three weeks before Christmas, but things were going well enough that we'd agreed to exchange presents. When he handed me the package, I knew that this was going very well—that he knew me well enough to know how much I'd appreciate a book. Any book.

He seemed nervous about it, though—until he unwrapped my present to him. Then, he started laughing. I'd given him a bottle of Klingon Blood Wine, purchased a few months prior at the just-about-to-close Star Trek: The Experience in Vegas. And he'd given me a book on the physics of Star Trek.

It was just one of the great magical moments from those early days of our relationship, the two of us discovering how much we had in common, how in sync we were. The kind of thing it hurts to remember now.

The Blood Wine never got opened; it sat on his wine rack for the next two and a half years. He's probably thrown it out by now. I'll never know. And I never finished reading the book—it still sits

on my bedside table, his first Christmas card to me serving as a bookmark. I don't remember the card's inscription perfectly—except for the part where he'd given up on finding anyone he could be with in Los Angeles, until he met me—and I can't bear to open it again.

As much as I might want to get rid of it, though, I'll keep this book always.

FADIMAN
Ex Libris: Confessions of a Common Reader

They had all left me a few months prior. They deserted me for higher education—I couldn't blame them.

We were Skyping when she told me that she had just bought a book on Amazon and shipped it to my house. I devoured the essays in a day.

Never before had I felt so thankful towards an author. Anne Fadiman brought my friends back home to me in a small, green book; she was one of us.

I bought every copy of *Ex Libris* I could find in Houston that Christmas. I gave it to the friends who hadn't read it, to my English teachers, and to strangers. I took two copies of it to college with me, both of which are currently lent out. I'm not sure if I'll ever get them back, but I'm more than happy to buy more.

I recommend this to any book lover I meet. I have made new friends along the way, for books are what help me bridge connections.

We are scattered all over the country, but my Library Kids will always sit on my bookshelf.

HOFSTADTER
Gödel, Escher, Bach

We were so young: junior high school young. He liked me, and while occasionally I'd look up when he made a joke, I did not reciprocate the feelings. We graduated and bumped into each other on the last day of junior high. He wrote in my yearbook and I wrote in his. That was that. Fast forward years later. Thanks to Facebook, we became friends and hung out. He was dating somebody special and when his last relationship fell apart, he called to chat. We remained platonic on both ends until he fell back into that romantic black hole for me. Unfortunately or fortunately, depending on how you view unrequited love, I still did not feel the same way about him.

He is not one to read, but he was engulfed in *GEB*. Esoteric, it was the marriage of science and music and art, in all of which he had so much potential but no drive. One day I expressed interest in borrowing his copy, but he said it was falling apart. A couple days later it arrived in an Amazon box with greetings of cheer on a piece of paper. I had decided to lend the copy to a boy I'd been seeing. And while deep down inside I know the book isn't for him, he's trying. The same way I know, deep down inside, I'll never reciprocate the same romantic notions for my friend. The boy decided to purchase his own copy of *GEB*. My copy is on the floor of my room; the interest for it has faded, or what little I had in the beginning vanished. As for the friend, this dance he's been doing with me for at least five years should end like my journey with *GEB*. I think it says a lot when somebody opens up his or her literary world to you and you have no interest in staying. I hope that, someday, some girl will want to stay in the world Hofstadter has created with my friend.

HESSE
Siddhartha

My boyfriend from the ages of sixteen to twenty-one was passionate about mountain bikes, playing the guitar, and me. In that order. Really. In order to get more face time with the guy, I picked up his interests, which meant that I obtained a six-hundred-dollar bike and cut my nails short to learn chords and finger-picking. I also scared the shit out of myself trying to jump creeks on trails in the woods, and tried to get used to the bloody lines that the crankset made on my calves. I thought that if I could master his hobbies, he would believe that I was just as valuable to his happiness as they were.

However, as we got older, his interests morphed, and I found myself coming second or third to rock-climbing, East Asian studies, and the culture of Scotland. Once again, I tried to pick up his interests. I bent my body into the impossible nooks and crags of a rock-climbing wall, tried to be interested when he discussed the benefits of Buddhism, and wished him bon voyage as he went off on a two-week college trip to Scotland, more excited than ever to be experiencing new things, especially those things (it felt at the time) that I had no way of experiencing with him.

In spite of spending all of this time and dough on developing the skill set he so desired for me to have, I still managed to retain one of my own interests, which was reading. He was never a big reader; his prepubescent bookshelf was mostly filled with flimsy Goose-bumps paperbacks that slowly drew in the occasional philosophy book or novel to keep them company. He understood my love of the written word but didn't share it.

When we broke up for a short time during my sophomore year of college, he sent me a package filled with things that he thought I would enjoy, as a gesture of good will, including *Siddhartha*. I could almost hear his voice as I flipped through the pages: "This is one of the most meaningful stories I have ever read. This story made me want to become a better person." He really was melodramatic, even for a nineteen-year-old.

At the time, I was delighted by the gifts and thought that it was so sweet of him to offer me a story that had had such a profound effect on his little adolescent heart. So I read it. I remember thinking that I couldn't connect with the story. Nothing about it spoke to me or my place in life. After three more years with the guy, I realized that this was symptomatic of our entire relationship. I realized that if I couldn't connect with a book that had changed his life, then I probably would never connect with him in the fundamental way that I wanted to.

Ending the five-year relationship was the most difficult thing I have ever attempted. Almost as bad as that V3 that gave me back spasms.

HESSE
Siddhartha

I was sixteen years old and he was my first love. He had long brown limbs, played tennis, didn't eat red meat, and was always on the honor roll. I was both attracted and intimidated by his brilliance. He was: physics, chemistry, advanced math. I was: Spanish, anthropology, and English literature. We use to hang out innocently after school, doing homework in the senior lounge, but sometimes we'd sneak out to the back of the school and make out in the tennis courts. One day he, also the son of a Brahmin, gave me his favorite book and I devoured it. Inside, he had inscribed a personal note: "You are my Kamala, the one I've been waiting for." I was both incredibly touched and turned on to be likened to Kamala, the courtesan who instructs Siddhartha on the art of physical love and becomes the mother of his child.

After graduation, we split up, with him moving to the U.S. and me to the UK to study. But despite time and distance, every summer vacation, when we traveled back home to see our families, we would inevitably meet and, unable to keep our hands off each other, fall in love all over again. It didn't work out in the end— long distance never usually does—but we remain friends till today. Every time I read a book about a young, brilliant, long-limbed Indian boy (and there are several), I am reminded of him, young love, and those hot summer days we spent together.

HEMINGWAY
The Sun Also Rises

We met in Athens. He was a Greek student studying American lit, and I was an American student writing Greek theater.

He couldn't believe that I hadn't read Hemingway, and he teased me about it the entire time I was there. I teased him about being an entitled anarchist. We did all of this teasing in front of my boyfriend of four years.

The teasing turned desperate and we took to hiding in elevators and wandering the city late at night. On my last night in town we drank ourselves stupid and gave in to our mutual desire.

I was running for the plane when he slipped me his tattered copy of *The Sun Also Rises* and I gave him a brand-new *Breakfast of Champions* that I had picked up in an English-language bookstore. In his inscription he likened me to Daffy Duck and left me a riddle that, if solved, would lead to his email address. I left him a hidden message on twenty-one Post-it notes strewn through his new paperback.

We solved the riddles and spent a few months sending feverish emails about love and destiny, but when I saw him months later, we couldn't look each other in the eye. He spent a week in the apartment that I shared with my boyfriend.

I was the spoiled, selfish woman and he was the rugged, drunken man.

We may not have lasted, but he introduced me to my one true love: Hemingway.

FITZGERALD
Tender is the Night

She raptured me in summer by giving me Fitzgerald's flawed and gorgeous masterpiece, the book that held his tortured heart. It changed my life.

An old, battered paperback, it had character. She bought it for me while we were in New Orleans down at the market on Bourbon Street. Her pale hair, the same color as the sunlight that day, streaming behind her, leaving particles behind on the wind. I was seventeen and she was eighteen and I could not imagine a creature more lovely. Her eyes stretching out forever like twin oceans. But she was leaving . . . she wanted to be a doctor and go to Africa. I wrote her poetry.

We were sorting through the bargain books when it caught her hand and swayed her. She lifted the tiny thing gently, looked inside, and stared at the blue cover. She smiled, an impression of her mouth, the lips going back and staying against her teeth.

A month later it was over—we had fractured because she had to leave and I couldn't bear to see her go. So I ran away. I read *Tender Is the Night* and wrote poems and poems and poems about her. I looked at photographs—love so fleeting, but so long, there and past but still here. I saw her once from a distance and was struck down with fear and awe; her eyes blazed and her head was halo bright. I wrote her a letter years later that said everything I'd ever felt. The book was in it. The book had more of her in it than it had a right to. "Nicole," I'd whisper or cry, half nostalgic, all drunk. You write songs to get over it, you write books. Fitzgerald. He knew.

She is gone, is vibrant as memory but nothing else. The book changed me. God save the book.

GAARDER
Sophie's World

You gave me the book and, after an ill-fated week, were too cowardly to ask for it back. The book was *Sophie's World* by Jostein Gaarder, and I read it in a loft at a lake in Virginia. It taught me a lot. You taught me little.

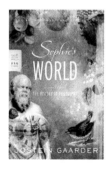

The Book of Mormon

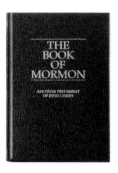

We met in a high school class. He was a year ahead of me. It wasn't a romance. No hint of that. It was a friendship—a friendship between a boy and a girl who were smarter than most of those around them, two teenagers starved for real intellectual discussions of the important questions—such as the meaning of life, the existence of god, the nature of existence, the importance of justice. We would talk for hours, discussing and disagreeing with conviction and passion. You know, the way one does when one is young and theory and ideology still hold redemptive promise. For Christmas my junior year he gave me the Book of Mormon. Yes, that Book of Mormon, the Mormon bible. He was a devout Mormon. I was a fervent atheist. At first I found his gift inappropriate and irritating. But I had grown up in Mormon country and knew the importance the church placed on proselytizing. I decided to accept the gift graciously and just appreciate my friend's good intentions. I never read the Book of Mormon, of course, but I kept it on my bookshelf nonetheless. After all, it was a gift from a friend. I lost track of him after he graduated. Three years later I ran into him. In a gay bar. He was there with his partner, his lover. He told me the whole story—how he had come out after high school, how his conservative Mormon parents and siblings had been open-minded enough to still love him and to accept his partner as a second son and brother. Then he told me that the Church of Latter-day Saints had excommunicated him. "How do you feel about that?" I asked, "I know how important the church is to you."

His response was, "How can I be part of a faith that can't accept me the way I am, the way God made me?"

A few months later I was packing to move apartments and ran across the Book of Mormon. I threw it in the trash.

WARREN
PostSecret: Confessions on Life, Death, and God

It was a gift from a very dear friend. I was struggling to do my best in college and dealing with the questions of faith that come with growing older. I wasn't sure how to look at the world without letting go of all that I had gathered in my twenty-two years. This book didn't answer my questions or calm my fears. However, something much more beautiful was realized—I'm not alone. The secrets poured from the book. Each one exciting, fearful, and completely understood. The secret that tugged at me was on the back cover: "I am a Christian who is falling in love with someone who doesn't believe in God . . . and I think it is a beautiful love story." With words like these, I found peace in my own misunderstandings and questions not yet answered.

TENGBOM
I Wish I Felt Good All the Time

My grandmother, knowing that at the age I was, I'd soon be heading into difficult years, sent me this book. It's a book of devotionals: short essays paired with a Bible verse and a prayer meant to offer guidance with a specific problem or issue in life.

So, as those storms came and went, I'd go to the shelf and pull this one down. And I tried. I really did. Tried to study, tried to believe, tried to find comfort in something that had given my grandparents so much peace throughout their lives. But for me, it didn't work.

I kept the book for years, and whenever I had a problem and I'd turn to my shelves for help, I'd slide my finger across the spine of this one and just leave it there. I don't even know when I got rid of it, or how. It's just gone, along with the promises it made. There is peace in books, but for me, there is no peace in that one.

RILKE
Letters to a Young Poet

He was my cousin and I barely knew him. I would have loved to, but he took his life and inadvertently left me his books instead. My best memory of him was our discussion of books, our love for information, and the like. I became like a sponge listening to him speak about books that I had heard about, books that made one cultured . . . until my younger brother interrupted us with some blabber about the latest video games. It was probably the last time we spoke.

He took his life two and a half years after his twin brother died in his sleep from an asthma attack. I swear it was like the opening of a hit list on my family. In those five or six years I lost three cousins, an aunt, and an uncle. But new additions to the family, loving support along with the small accomplishment of just waking up in the morning, helped me heal. When his older sister was getting married, my sister and I were in the wedding party, so we were going to Boston, our first time there since his funeral. His mom reluctantly decided to stay in the same house he had committed suicide in. It was extra eerie at first because we slept in his room. Time, however, dulled the ominous feeling, plus they had removed most of his possessions, and for that I was grateful.

The day before we left, V, his sister, decided to spend the night at the house, too. She had been asked to finally throw away his books, and I jumped out of bed. I walked over to her and silently begged her not to. They weren't many, two of my duffel bags could have carried them, but they were filled with our clothes and shoes. I told V that I'd take some—whatever I could carry. One book in particular stood out like a sore heart and I leaped at it. Rainer Maria Rilke's *Letters to a Young Poet,* a captivating read. It tackled loneliness and self-fulfillment as if they were friends and not the tumultuous journeys that everyone must trek. It was beautiful and I believe it was the last book he read. I can speculate about how he interpreted the book, but only my testimony of it will suffice.

Rilke celebrates isolation not as a jail or self-inflicted choking pain but the path to knowing the inner person. It's not just for writers or readers. It's for life, period. Handwritten notes and Post-its were tucked between the pages. The book was a gift from a close friend. Maybe they saw the alienation my cousin was desperately trying to hide. Maybe it pushed him into his downfall or gave him a misleading hope in an early death. I will never know, but I do know he left more than books; he left me a renewal of my life. I'm fighting to fill the voids I have in my heart. I keep in mind that life is a journey, we are never truly alone and even though each day is a struggle . . . it is well with my soul.

KRAKAUER
Under the Banner of Heaven

There was a little old man in the coffee shop/bookstore I worked at in Boston. I made coffee, he sorted books. I can't remember his name, but I do remember his surprising knowledge of pop culture as well as obscure subjects, such as my religion. Being raised in a strict Mormon home, and subsequently choosing to leave the church once I found out about its dark and secret past, it was hard to find people who really understood how hard a transition it was. However, he knew all about the church. After sitting down and discussing the deeper doctrines for a few hours, he recommended *Under the Banner of Heaven* to help me feel less alone in my decision. "One second!" he said, and disappeared into the rows of tall oak shelves. He emerged only moments later with the book in his hands. "Here!" he said breathlessly, with a smile. "I hope this helps."

It was quite a depressing book, focusing more on polygamy in the fundamentalist or FLDS church, but he was right; it really did help. Reading of the heinous acts performed in the name of the

LDS church affirmed that I had made the right decision. I felt inexplicably strengthened by reading of these atrocities, knowing that I escaped and could now educate others. Besides being informative, it was beautifully written and now has a fixed place on my bookshelf, waiting patiently to be given to the right person who needs it like I did.

ANTHONY
The Source of Magic

When we first moved in together, he handed over all his sci-fi and fantasy novels, professing Piers Anthony his favorite. I'd read some of Anthony's other books and enjoyed them, and tore through the Xanth novels, starting with *The Source of Magic*. (He'd lost the first book, and to this day, I've never read it.) At first, I was enamored with this lone author we shared; I, the lit major and he, the hard-core science geek finally had something in common. I giggled over the humor and tried to get him to read books I loved, too. But as the years went on and he read no more fiction, I realized he was just like those novels: stuck in the teen-boy land of jokes about panties and not wanting to grow up and take on responsibilities.

BROOKS
The Zombie Survival Guide

She gave me this book when she was about to leave for a new job overseas. I thought it was a present of love, but our love was already dead. A few months later we broke up. My blindness to the truth was what gave "life" to our dead love, in those final few months.

But it wasn't real love; it was zombie love.

AUSTEN & GRAHAME-SMITH
Pride and Prejudice and Zombies

He gave me this.

It didn't last.

ANTUNES
Knowledge of Hell

This relationship was doomed from the start, I think, and not only because we were so different, but because we tried to bridge that gap. She wanted me in her world (which was loneliness, misanthropy, tension, impeccable style) and I wanted her to come out to the world. We thought we had made it for some time. She gave me this book (its Greek translation) during summer vacation. And maybe I read  too much into it, but at the time I thought it revealed her sweeter, lighter, more humane side. It's an intense book, but it's not a lesson for a life in which mellowness is weakness, and good-natured humour plain old silliness. I thought this was her being more lowkey. Along with the other scribblings on the margins, she'd written *"Surtout pas d'emotion"* in the last page. When her primary mode, direct, tense confrontation gave way to her secondary mode of communication, irony, she'd write things like that. I think that's the endnote to our relationship as a whole: "Above all, without emotion," that is, always with emotion, with all the emotion in the world. Antunes's fever-dream writing is a pretty good emulation: a sizzling, smoking streak cutting through air, one-note, monomaniacal, obsessive, sweet, and loving, without asking for anything back, or for everything back. I read it again and all I could picture was our battered, bitten, reddened skin, our breath running out, our words, veering into nonsense, trying to build something which would not, could not stand because mortar and earthquakes are the worst friends. We broke up spectacularly, and by that I mean sadly, but with the pretense of spectacle, and then she found someone with whom she could synchronize herself, and I think she's been happy ever since.

BURROUGHS
Magical Thinking

We were two obnoxious high school students who had been coaxed and convinced that we had a sort of gifted intelligence. We threw ourselves into an elite intellectual circle in our small community and constantly attempted to one-up one another as we tried to prove that the label we were branded with since elementary school was not an ill-informed mistake.

We took up reading books together. We tried to stretch our minds further than our small school would allow us and extended our knowledge through thousands of pages of unassigned reading.

We picked up only Pulitzer Prize winners and philosophy books, as we thought these texts had that all-important stamp of intellectual approval. We raced through *Sophie's World, The Brief Wondrous Life of Oscar Wao,* philosophy primers, and *The Interpreter of Maladies* all in a competition to see who could read each text fastest and create the most academic analysis. Yes. We were completely obnoxious.

Before winter break we exchanged gifts. I gave him a carefully selected collection of Kafka. He gave me *Magical Thinking,* almost telling me to slow down to take a cerebral breath and to stop trying so hard. I gladly took the text and was completely surprised at what it contained, not prepared for humorous anecdotes and layers of self-deprecation. My angsty high school self analyzed why he had selected that text to give me, launching me into a tormented state.

We broke up a week after I read it. We were too competitive and too unbearable. It would take until our second semester of college to lose the intellectual hubris.

Now I leaf through the book occasionally for fun and reminisce upon the days where I thought proving my intelligence was far more important than the blossoming relationship.

BLAKE
The Complete Poetry and Prose of William Blake

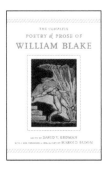

He, lovelorn literary loser, just like me—but better at even that than I was, for I was a mere apprentice—gave me a hardcover edition of the complete poems of William Blake.

I'd brought him to the legendary Powell's in Hyde Park, Chicago, and the Blake edition was on my shopping list. I was back in school at thirty-four, newly divorced, to finish the BA in English literature I should have taken the first time around.

Starry-eyed, in love with the man and the poems, I found the book, but sadly noted its seventy-dollar price tag. I slid it back onto the shelf and pulled down another copy, a shopworn softcover that was only fifteen dollars. He took it from me, put it back, and took down the pristine hardcover, clasping it to his chest like the treasure it is.

"Will you let me buy it for you?" he asked, his eyes shining. I did.

ALLEN & GREENOUGH
New Latin Grammar

I was studying Latin and dying to get a copy of Allen and Greenough's *New Latin Grammar*, the classic for serious students for over a hundred years. But I only wanted it in hardcover; the paperback was a flimsy reprint that would fall apart with little use, and this was an important reference book that I would use forever. I always preferred reading hardcovers, even if they were just airport novels.

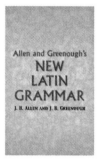

Allen and Greenough's
**NEW
LATIN
GRAMMAR**
J. B. ALLEN AND J. B. GREENOUGH

I mentioned my desire to get it. A few weeks later she proudly gave me a present, and I unwrapped it to find a copy of the paperback. "I tracked it down for you," she said. I stared at her and then flipped it straight into the garbage. She was outraged, and we had a huge fight. She said that she had bought it for me with love because she knew I wanted it, and how could I be so cruel. I said she should have known that I only wanted the hardcover, that I could have found the paperback in four different bookstores around campus, but I was holding out for the one that mattered, and that she didn't understand me at all if she thought I would be happy with the paperback.

It took us three more months to break up.

ERDRICH
Love Medicine

The only right thing about T was what he gave me for Christmas: *Love Medicine,* by Louise Erdrich. Inside the front cover he wrote, "Maybe one day you'll write a beautiful book like this."

We had started dating that November. I was twenty and had been on exactly one date. He was a twenty-five-year-old film student. On paper we looked great together. Both Chinese American, writerly, and from New Jersey. Even our family backgrounds were similar, our parents part of that generation who, as children, fled mainland China and the Communists for Taiwan.

But in person he made me nervous. He had the habit of gazing at not just me, but everyone, with a small curious smile, and saying suddenly things like, "Tell me about a dream you had," and "What are you thinking right now? Right at this moment?" My mind always went blank when he asked me these things, and I'd answer, "Nothing."

That winter I caught a cold, which left me with a long, lingering cough. "You need some tea," he'd always say. But I coughed more out of anxiety than sickness. My stomach would twist and I'd cough to the point of gagging.

Still, I told him he could take my virginity. He declined. "I don't want to hurt you," he said, although even then I knew it wouldn't be him who'd hurt me.

I read *Love Medicine* that Christmas break and he was right: it was a beautiful book, and I wanted to write one like it. A story like that started stirring in my head, a story about leaving, about the desert, about finding a lost someone. About missing someone you never knew.

We broke up that January. "I don't think I can fall in love with you," he said, not unkindly. "What about you?"

"I don't know," I said. "I have no idea." I stopped coughing after that.

GOODKIND
Wizard's First Rule

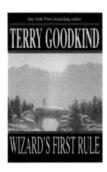

My best friend told me she never saw this coming, never thought I would break this one rule as cleanly as I did. She warned me that he was in love, much too deeply to not be dangerous.

"Just the way he looks at you, like you are the whole universe," she said. She warned me to be careful, that I was going to break his heart.

"I know," I said. "I am just trying to be happy for as long as I can be."

It wasn't long. And it wasn't his heart that got broken.

EGGERS
A Heartbreaking Work of Staggering Genius

So I started dating this girl based on a conversation we had while working on a show—she's a Kindle reader and I'm strictly a physical copy man.

For my birthday, she gave me a copy of *A Heartbreaking Work of Staggering Genius,* telling me that it was her favorite book and I was going to love it.

I broke up with her three days later, and now, having finally gotten to the book two months after the breakup, I realize I made the right decision.

FAULKNER
Light in August

Always an avid reader, my lover was not. Shortly before I planned on leaving the Midwest for school in the South, he lent me the copy of *Light in August* he'd painstakingly annotated in AP literature. As the only book he ever gave me, something highlighting many of the negative aspects of the South was not exactly the romantic gesture I would have liked. Even so, I held on to his book for many years, but never managed to read it.

After four years as an English major, I've read far more Faulkner than my former beau ever will. I don't regret leaving him behind the first time. But for a lover that I continually find myself drawn to, some part of me wishes I could stop leaving him behind. Now, after developing a healthy appreciation for Faulkner, I know I should read *Light in August,* but some part of me feels like that would be accepting the end of our time together.

BITTMAN
How to Cook Everything: The Basics

We started dating in the winter, just after the holidays in cold Massachusetts. On one of our first dates, she cooked dinner in her kitchen, and right away I was at her employ with preparation. I lacked her mastery, though. I baked her vegan cupcakes for Valentine's Day, and they were as good as hockey pucks, sitting solid and cold in the bottom of the cupcake tin. The next weekend I attempted to make surprise risotto, but she had to step in and take over cooking it.

I love a passionate girl, and she was passionate about cooking. She even filmed herself cooking barley risotto in the college kitchen for one of her courses, while I sat in the living room next door, in a completely irrational panic attack. We both had our neuroses, but we shared many wonderful meals together, with me doing what I could to help prepare.

Bittman's book was a gift from her on my birthday, and it has been well used. I eventually became a bit more proficient with cooking, and love many of the simple recipes. Cracking it open today still reminds me of cooking meals together with her. If only maintaining a healthy relationship was as easy as homemade macaroni and cheese . . .

How to Cook
Everything

the **basics**

simple recipes anyone can cook

Mark Bittman

BISHOP
The Complete Poems 1927–1979

He met me during my summer of spontaneity. I was jobless and in an unfamiliar city. He was preparing to graduate from the local university. We got together the night before I had to leave for home, and three days before his lease was up. It was inconvenient timing.

That night we exchanged books, expecting to trade books once again the next time we saw each other. We were both English majors and we communicated best through writing. Yet it was easier to connect to each other through the writing of others.

The last day we exchanged books, he handed me a copy of *The Complete Poems 1927–1979* of Elizabeth Bishop. He ended things two weeks later. I hadn't even had the opportunity to crack the spine of the book.

It sat on my shelf for over a month, like an undeserved trophy. I couldn't bring myself to read it. I still don't know if there was some warning sign contained in the pages.

I did everything I could to give him back his book. A month later I returned it through a friend of a friend.

I hid a note between the pages of the poem "One Art" so even if there was a subtle message he was trying to give me, he would at least get his book back full of real meaning.

MILNE
Winnie-the-Pooh

Even though, as children of the seventies, we grew up immersed in Disney's charms—I, for instance, had a Pooh-themed first birthday party and have the photos to prove it—neither of us had ever actually read the stories. At some point between marriage and having babies, when we were still dreamy and in love, he bought the books and we began to read them together, aloud, one chapter per night, just before bed.

They were far sweeter and sadder than we'd anticipated. Piglet reaches for Pooh's hand, saying, "I just wanted to be sure of you." Piglet was articulate and thoughtful, while Pooh was really concerned with lunch. Piglet said, "We'll be Friends Forever, won't we, Pooh?" and Pooh answered: "Even longer."

That turned out not to be true.

MURKOFF & MAZEL
What to Expect When You're Expecting

He was my sweetheart all through high school. Not much of a reader, but a hopeless romantic, always leaving notes and presents in my locker. We had very different plans for life after high school; he was enlisting and I was going to college. He had your typical fantasy: a house with a white picket fence where he would come home to dinner on the table and children there to greet him. I wanted to chain myself to trees in the rain forests of Brazil. It was easy to put these things away when we were in high school; I mean, why worry about what's happening in four years when we have now and we love each other?

The day before I was set to move into my dorm, he came to my house and gave me this book. I was speechless as I opened it, wondering what he meant by it. His chicken-scratch handwriting on the inside cover: "We're going to get married and have babies. You are my one and only."

I knew at that moment that we could not be together. What was real had been made into a fantasy by time and false hope.

When I looked up from the book, he was on one knee, with a ring (it was really just a piece of costume jewelry) in his hand.

He took the book with him when he stormed out of my house. We haven't spoken since.

HEMINGWAY
The Sun Also Rises

He didn't give the book to me, so much as I never gave it back.

I needed it to write a research paper; he needed it because it completed his special edition boxed set of Hemingway novels.

When he left, I hid it so he couldn't take it on his way out.

Every time I see it sitting on my shelf, I smile knowing my bookshelf is one fuller, and his boxed set is one short.

HELLER
Something Happened

We bonded over this book. In the midst of my ugly divorce, he recommended it as a case study in exactly how bad things can get. I think this was meant to be comforting, somehow. I bought it, read it, shuddered, and we went on.

Just before he broke up with me, I found a signed first edition in a used bookshop for five dollars. On the phone with him, later, I told him that I'd bought it for him. He said, "Why?" Just a few weeks later, it was all over.

HELLER
Catch-22

After hearing that *Catch-22* was my favorite novel of all time, my fiancé scoured used bookstores to find me a hardcover copy. This required effort and commitment in the days before eBay, you know. This remains my most favorite present he ever gave me, and a much more romantic Valentine than flowers or chocolate. I saved the handwritten receipt, showing he bought it on February 10, 1996. There's also a handwritten signature from a previous owner and the year 1975 noted inside the front cover.

FLYNN
Another Bullshit Night in Suck City

I had just met him and when I told him I was working the next week monitoring the summer storage room at our college, he said he would lend me a book. He gave me *Another Bullshit Night in Suck City* by Nick Flynn, because it was about working in a Boston homeless shelter, and working with the homeless was something he had done all through college. He wanted me to read the book so I had an idea what it was like. I read the whole thing in a week, sitting on the cold floor of this huge room while moving-out students filled it with boxes, and I slowly began to learn more about him. By the end, I was so in love with him and so desperate to have any excuse to talk to him that I slipped a photo of myself and my mom in between the pages when I gave the book back. Just in case, if we lost touch, I could say "Hey, I used this picture of me and my mom as a bookmark, and I think I left it in the book . . ."

That was five years ago. Two months ago we got married. The photo is still in the book.

HAY
A Student of Weather

I met him on the Internet. Not something so simple as eHarmony or the like, but through blogs. First there were comments, then emails, phone calls, text messages, an airline ticket, *plans*. Finding ways of saying "I love you" without saying "I love you." Late nights, a meeting of minds. Falling asleep to the sound of his voice, miles away.

When we finally met in person, nothing was right. I couldn't stop loving the man I had built in my mind instead of the one across from me at a table or next to me on the couch. There was disappointment, then bickering, fighting, another airline ticket, *silence*.

For my birthday he had bought me a used copy of *A Student of Weather* by Elizabeth Hay because I had just finished *Late Nights on Air* and loved it.

Later he sent me a letter saying he regretted nothing. I keep it in the book along with a pressed flower from the bouquet he gave me at the airport, when we were still brimming with hope.

It's been years but I haven't read the book yet. I think I'm afraid to.

GELARDI
Born to Rule

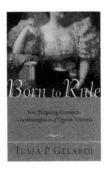

He, an occasional reader (mainly sci-fi); and I, the diehard reader. We met right after my ex and I broke up. A few months later he asked me out and I said no. "I just want to be single for a while," I told him. So for the next three years he was persistent. I kept turning him down and he would just say, "You know it's going to happen, just accept it." Then finally he asked and I said yes. So, a few months after, Christmas came along and I briefly mentioned my love of English royal history. As I opened up to this novel, in that moment I knew he was my other. A year later and we're getting our first apartment together.

KING
The Dark Tower

I was drawn to his passion—the way he took each breath in deliberately, the way his eyes held me close as if I were a loved one. He recited entire poems from memory, scribbled lines for me on folded sheets, and spoke in a borrowed manner that made him seem like a secret. I wanted to unfold him.

I wasn't sure why he liked me. At twenty-one, I was reserved, perpetually nervous, and uncomfortable with myself unless I was alone. I liked reading. I loved books—their shape, their magic, the way they made me feel more alive. We shared that.

We stumbled upon each other unexpectedly and in the throes of terrible timing, entangled in the arms of our pasts; our relationship reflected this gracelessly. It was many months until I discovered that what I'd seen as endearing mysteriousness was simply stark confusion. Haunted and hurting, the boy I was in a relationship with was lost at sea.

We had been involved for a year when he gave me his copy to

read. I was skeptical when he introduced me to the series; I didn't share his affinity for King, but after a few chapters, I was lost inside the world he knew so well. I consumed the first few books with a strange sort of hunger—I found the lines he had written months before, words that had laced his lips on their way to me, thoughts that I had assumed to be raw, genuinely his. I learned more about him through these books than he had ever revealed to me himself, but mostly I began to understand one thing: like Roland of Gilead, my boy was on a quest of his own. He was searching for something—something to calm the wild seas, something to make him whole and alive—but that something wasn't me. I knew it long before I would allow myself to say it aloud. We broke up on my birthday, disappointment filling my heart with a weight much more hollow than sadness.

It took me two more years to get through the series. I allowed months to float like icebergs between each book, finding less and less of a reason to accompany anyone on a journey intended to be undergone alone. I finished book seven swiftly only to be surprised by my own reaction, disappointment filling my heart with a weight much heavier than sadness.

HASS
Sun Under Wood

We had met in a writing workshop and we'd sit for hours talking poetry. I thought him a legend. Months later I was felled by a terrible case of the flu and my parents had left me in hospital quarantine—they being paranoid and it being the season of swine flu—without reading material or a method by which to contact friends. I was going stir-crazy, rereading the daily paper from beginning to end, even scrutinizing the labels of my medicine bottles.

On the fourth day of my confinement, my lover walked into my hospital room. I hadn't told him where I was, but he overheard enough from my friends to know which hospital I was in. He had asked for me at every floor. We kissed, stupidly, through our required surgical masks. He expressed dismay at the dull view from the window, commented on the lack of sunlight, and told me he couldn't bring me flowers but he did bring me a book by my favorite poet. In a way, it saved my life.

It's been years since we were lovers, but he hasn't returned to claim it. I like to think it's mine.

KHAYYÁM
The Rubaiyat of Omar Khayyám

When he gave me the book, I was thirteen, he ten years older. A slim volume printed on thick parchment paper, a poem written by a man with a name like a poem: Omar Khayyám. Inside were verses in quatrains, and black-and-white line drawings that suggested rather than showed those lineaments of gratified desire more often sought than found by the very young. I wanted him to kiss me but he would not; instead he gave me the book.

"You're going to be a poet some day," he said.

"But how can I ever become a poet if no one will kiss me?"

"You're like a Botticelli Madonna," he said.

"What's that?" I said.

"You'll find out . . ."

Reading it took my breath away, as much as any kiss ever could. "A Book of Verses underneath the Bough, A Jug of Wine, a Loaf of Bread—and Thou." This sort of thing works when you're just thirteen. It gave me gold and purple dreams, it gave me words I could taste like butter and honey, it gave me the shivers.

Later he kissed me after all. Later, much later, I found out he'd been sleeping with my mother.

TOLKIEN
The Hobbit

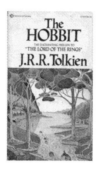

When I was eight, my favorite aunt gave me a book. She said it was one of her favorites and promised I'd love it. But, try as I did, I dreaded the book and never read beyond the first page. I was intimidated by what I thought I'd find inside: little knights and trolls, armor and magic and no girl characters at all. There is something about being recommended books by people who don't really know me well. It feels so uncomfortable, an imposition of sorts. There are few people whose word about a book I can take unquestioningly. But, likewise, my recommendations to others always seem to miss the mark. A book may remind me powerfully of someone, but when I describe it to them, they don't sound interested.

So I carried the book with me as we moved house to house, installing it dutifully on my shelf alongside my real favorites. It stood in mute castigation, its spine staring at me reproachfully as I moved it this way and that to slide in some Wilde or Austen, Dickens or Hardy. I felt such guilt over that book. I mean, really,

I couldn't even try? Couldn't even open it up and see? Everybody else raved about it. My aunt would ask me each time I saw her what I thought of it, and I had to admit I still hadn't read it.

Finally, probably ten years later, spurred on by a new boyfriend who adored Tolkien, I read it. And . . . meh. I was right. It didn't captivate me intellectually or emotionally. I finished it, then tried its more intense cousins, but to this day, I would reread *Jane Eyre* or *Sister Carrie* before opening Tolkien again. As my aunt said, many years after she gave me the book, I am a city girl, and this book is not of the city.

•

RAWICZ
The Long Walk:
The True Story of a Trek to Freedom

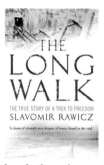

Her grandma lent this to her and then she gave it to me. In musical tastes we're soul mates, listening to Cole Porter or The Who at the same time as each other and not ever realizing it. I stayed the night at her house and she lent me this book the next day, telling me she stayed up all night in the summer reading it. I was pleased because, despite my voracious reading habits, nobody had ever given or lent me a book they themselves had loved.

This book is beyond depressing and I never finished it. I can somehow deal with the existential depression of Camus, but the real-life sorrows and pain endured within this book just felt too real to me. I had no stomach for it. I couldn't understand how my friend, with whom I stayed up till three a.m. talking about everything under the sun, could enjoy such a miserable read.

She's my best friend and I've lent her books which she's read, which makes me feel guilty for not trying very hard on this one. But whatever. It's only a book.

Anyway, my dad took the book and loved it. I haven't given it back to her yet and her grandma is wondering what happened to it.

SPILLANE
The Long Wait

When I was twelve, my uncle Charlie introduced me to Mickey Spillane. I loved the first-person, tough guy narration. The character's fearlessness and appeal to women were qualities that I lacked. *The Long Wait* was not a Mike Hammer book, but I soon discovered Hammer and read all the titles. At the stationery store in my suburban strip mall, Spillane paperbacks featured half-naked women on the covers and I was nervous that they wouldn't sell them to me.

Uncle Charlie drove a 7Up truck in New York City, and as a teenager I'd work as his helper during school vacations. This was in the 1970s, when the prostitutes roamed the sidewalks in daylight. Mike Hammer lived and worked in Manhattan and I got a kick out of being part of the same city.

Uncle Charlie retired and moved to Florida with my aunt in 1979, the year I graduated from high school. Ten years later, working as a book publicist for Dutton, Spillane's original publishers, I met Mickey Spillane. Spillane had just written his first Mike Hammer novel in nineteen years, and he had come to New York to do publicity. We went out to dinner and I had him sign a book for Uncle Charlie.

At ninety-four, Uncle Charlie still lives in Florida, and he's in good shape. He drives, shops, and shoots pool. At four p.m., he has a martini, the same ritual he had back in the 1970s, when New York City was Mike Hammer's town.

EVANOVICH
One for the Money

Traditionally, they are released every June, right before my birthday. One novel each year, a remarkable pace for any writer. Summoning some tact, I'll say they're not the sort of thing I usually read. At all. But once she'd persuaded me to read the first one, I grudgingly admitted they were rather fun, and I quickly caught up to the latest release. From then on, she gave me the latest adventure of Stephanie Plum as a birthday gift every year. Until 2009. *Finger Lickin' Fifteen.* (I assume some fried chicken is consumed during the course of the novel; knowing Stephanie and Lula's ravenous tastes for junk food, I'm not surprised.)

That year, a month before my birthday, I told her son we needed to divorce. She didn't give me a book that year. In fact, she never spoke to me again. She had been my second mother for seventeen years, and I never saw her again. I left the books in his house when I moved out. I doubt either of them know how much they meant to me.

ALBOM
Tuesdays with Morrie

This particular book was given to me not in physical, but in spoken form.

I had met this girl a few months earlier, and she turned out to be just the person I needed at that time—a person who supported me and gave me back my self-confidence. We're no longer in a relationship, but she's one of my closest friends.

One night she started reading this book to me. She'd read a couple of pages every night, and it soon became something I looked forward to during the day. The main story of the book is quite sad, and it's probably not a book I'd pick up myself since I don't read too much. But I'm very happy she read it to me, and I wouldn't want to be without our relationship or this book.

Thank you. I'll always hold you in high regard because of this one.

JONES
Light Boxes

He contacted me out of the blue, sending a message through the Goodreads site. I'm not sure why he reached out to me; I was not, and am not an active user on the site. He mentioned that based on the types of books I read I might be interested in reading his new book, *Light Boxes*. The premise about a town battling the month of February instantly appealed to me. The problem was, I was new to New York and didn't quite know how to go about finding a book that Barnes & Noble wasn't selling (don't worry, I've learned my lesson). He offered to send me a copy and refused to let me send him a check. It was delivered to my office because I was too afraid to give out my real address to a stranger. He signed the inside title page.

It is a slim little book and for a few hours on the night I received it I was completely absorbed in their world. I was captivated by the town's story of fighting off the month of February and all the side effects that come with that month. I promised myself to make a tradition of reading it each February.

That next February I found myself slowly working my way through *Anna Karenina*. I finished that book on a sunny Sunday morning while sitting on my roof. The day was uncharacteristically warm and felt almost like spring. I decided to start *Light Boxes* right away, though I couldn't reconcile this tale of sadness and despair with day around me. I was just a few pages in when I got a call. When I got The Call. It's surprising how right the movies can get that moment. My knees buckled as I was told that my best friend had been hit by a car, hit by someone who didn't see fit to stop. Her condition was unknown.

I carried the book with me in those early days when we camped out at the hospital. The stories of townspeople standing in circles trying to make sense of things reminded me of the way we stood in waiting rooms, the way we stood around her bed. The many remedies they came up with to beat the effects of February made me think of all the ways I had tried and failed at fighting a sadness I couldn't shake when she didn't wake up.

The book carried me through those days. When I read it again last year, a year after the accident, I saw the story through the eyes of a woman who has weathered a season of sadness. In a few days I will start rereading this story that, though familiar, seems to shift and change with every rereading. When I open the book I will say a quiet thank-you to the author who, for reasons unknown, decided one day to send me this book.

SATERSTROM
The Pink Institution

A. came by my company's booth at a publishing conference in Chicago several years ago. I flipped through our catalog with him, his face mere inches from mine. I waxed poetic about our design practices and amazing authors. About an hour later he stopped by and dropped off a postcard from his university. He walked away, and it wasn't until he was out of sight that I turned the card over and read "Blues Bar? [and phone number]" We met up and spent every minute we could together over the weekend, from wrapping him in my peacoat in a park at one a.m. as we groped and kissed each other to keep warm, to him bearing witness to the euphoria of my first snow. On our last day at the conference he bought this book for me, from an author he adored. Written on the inside cover was "For M., a man even more beautiful and impressive than this story.—A." On the plane back home, I immediately devoured the story, a novel of meditations and prose poems, all linked by the narrator's fierce and macabre consciousness. It was the perfect memento of that tryst: raw and passionate, devoured in an instant, and leaving me wanting more.

ROBERTSON
Fresh from the Vegetarian Slow Cooker

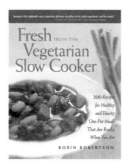

I was freshly divorced and my kids were gamely shuffling between our old house and my new apartment. They wanted to make me happy, and one day while we were at the grocery store, the younger one plucked this off a shelf and stuck it in my cart. I paid for it myself, but my son choosing it for me was strangely adult. He seemed to be saying, "You'll need this, Mom, to take care of yourself." And I do.

LANGENSCHEIDT
Taschenwörterbuch: Englisch-Deutsch, Deutsch-Englisch

Our dad had moved over a few months before, and after a long and exciting wait, we were arriving in Germany to join him in our new life there. He met us at the airport, our daddy, warm and familiar, smelling of the English Leather cologne my sister gave him for Christmas every year. In the car, he sternly told us we had to wear seat belts because it was the law here, and he twisted in his seat to hand this book back to me. I'd memorized the entire Berlitz phrase book, but this book was like a key to a new language, a new world. We only moved there because his job demanded it, but living in Europe imprinted in me a need for the foreign, for a cosmopolitan life. I live in New York City now, a decision my parents don't quite understand, but I can trace it all back to the wonders of the foreign, the joy in deciphering strange codes, in making the unfamiliar familiar. It's because of this book.

FERRIS
Then We Came to the End

Our workplace had gone sour. It only takes one bad apple, one asshole, to ruin a great vibe and make one's work life hell. Our bad apple was festering, lashing out with every fiber of her vicious being whenever she thought the bosses weren't looking. We liked the job, though, and my colleague stuck it out as long as possible before pulling the escape cord. In the meantime, she shared this book with me: a tale of work, of the ridiculous crap we go through to earn a living in this world. I'm still in the job. I'll hold on. I need the work!

CHILD, BERTHOLLE, BECK
Mastering the Art of French Cooking

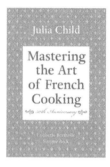 

Before the Julia Child resurgence, this set was hard to find. My mother-in-law, an avid home cook, guarded her original copy from the sixties. It occupied a place of pride in her kitchen: on display on the shelves alongside a bottle of Dom Pérignon she was saving for something or other. And one Christmas, under the tree sat a heavy, wrapped block: a beautiful two-volume boxed set for me. But I have never been as studious as she, and I just page through, getting ideas, before closing the cookbook and improvising. I appreciate the book, though . . . an attempt to share something that brought her great joy.

HODGES
Harbrace College Handbook

This was my dad's, and he bought it when I was a toddler, when he was taking some college courses in an attempt to advance at work. It was always around the house, and when I hit high school and had a lot of writing to do, he passed it on to me. In those days I'd sit in front of my electric typewriter, marveling at those twenty-six keys and all they could be when combined in the right ways, in magical ways. All that from just twenty-six little symbols. As I began to realize I might be a writer, I used this book to guide me, shaping my raw instinct into something structured, something fine and powerful.

It's hopelessly outdated now—today I use the *Chicago Manual* and Diana Hacker's *A Writer's Reference,* but I'll never get rid of this book, or my sense of wonder at what these twenty-six keys (they're MacBook keys now) can let me create.

BYATT
Possession

Back in college, she'd just finished it in a feverish marathon. She was supposed to be preparing for a chemistry exam, as I recall, but instead she was glued to this. She explained the plot to me rapturously, her eyes starry. And she pressed the book into my hands. I never read it. I kind of didn't need to—I saw it through her eyes and that was joy enough for me.

GERSHWIN
Ira Gershwin: Selected Lyrics

He was a musician, a jazz trumpeter. We dated for a few weeks, but with only tepid interest once we'd gotten over the initial burst of attraction. During that time, though, he waxed rhapsodic about the music he loved and gave me this book in an attempt to share that with me. Funny thing is, he was right. He awakened in me an interest in the music my grandparents loved. It's weird what you can take away from a relationship that might otherwise be called a failure. It wasn't a failure at all.

FISHER
The Art of Eating

I discovered M.F.K. Fisher quite by accident while working at a bookstore and devoured everything by her I could find. This was pre-Internet, pre-eBay. If you wanted an obscure book, you had to do some footwork or put in a special order at a real bookstore.

My boyfriend's mother was a great cook and loved to entertain, so I thought she'd love this book. She'd never heard of Fisher, but loved to read, so I was sure she'd love this. And she was going in for some minor surgery, so I thought she'd want something great to read while she recovered. She thanked me and, weeks later, handed the book back with its spine broken, reeking of cigarette smoke. I asked her what she thought of it and she shrugged. I was disappointed, of course, but I later learned how hard it was to earn her approval. She never gave it to me.

DOYLE
The Collected Sherlock Holmes

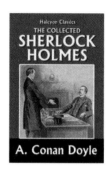

My brother is only three years younger than I am and we both love to read, which means we end up sharing a lot of books. Usually, since I am older, I buy books and he ends up reading them later on. But this time, he picked the book and I read it before he did. This series is very interesting because Sherlock continues to amaze everyone else by solving problems that, if other people thought about them for a long while, they *might* figure out. But Sherlock solves them in mere minutes. Most of the crimes are solved by Sherlock reading the perpetrator's body language and noticing details that allow him to deduce who was the real criminal. But he can't do any of this without his assistant, Dr. John Watson, who is older than he is. My brother was Sherlock and I was his Watson. He made the discovery, but I'm the one who benefited most.

MURAKAMI
Norwegian Wood

He was my English teacher and I, his favorite student. He said I should read it because of the strength it had. I didn't know what he was talking about until I turned the page and realized I had finished the book. He was right.

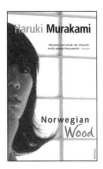

KAFKA
Die Verwandlung

He bought this for me in Berlin, knowing my German isn't too awful, that I'd be able to read it even if it took the help of a dictionary to do it. And that alone is a vote of confidence from one of the very few people who ever vote my way, one of the only people who stands on my side.

Yellow Pages

When I moved to Chicago, I was lost. I got the job at the last possible minute, right before the semester was to start. I took the apartment after talking with the landlord on Craigslist, and I sent her over to check it out and report back. She was also there to pick up my keys, and when I arrived at last, she had stocked the fridge with some water and juice and the cupboards with a box of cereal and a few borrowed dishes. She made sure there was a roll of toilet paper and a bar of soap in the bathroom, and in one corner of the tiny room, she placed this book in case I needed it, with a stack of local takeout menus tucked inside. It was an old-fashioned touch, but considering I couldn't afford Internet at home, it turned out to be a useful one.

I've never had a better friend and I hope I am as good to her as she is to me.

JOYCE
A Portrait of the Artist as a Young Man

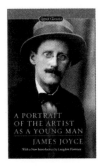

In high school we were clandestine friends. After school, we'd hang out, talk for hours, drive downtown to walk the streets, lurk in parks at dusk, go to art galleries. We'd pool our money for cups of coffee and meager dinners. He confided in me, and I in him. At school, though, it was a different story. I wasn't cool enough, too much an outsider for him to take a chance at identifying with me. If we were known to be close, people might start to question him, dig too deeply and scratch into the surface he'd constructed. I felt slighted, cheated, but he was all I had. I couldn't afford to let him go.

We were asked to choose a book and write a paper on it. I chose Maugham's *Of Human Bondage*. He chose *A Portrait of the Artist as a Young Man*. After we'd turned in our papers, we exchanged books. The choices, twenty years later, seem strangely apt. We were in bondage, of a type, afraid of bullies and disapproval. We were artists. We were young. These books could have been about us. They could have been by us.

DREISER
Sister Carrie

She always knows what I'd like to read. Sometimes her guesses are off the mark; sometimes she engages in wild experiments or flights of fancy based on something as intangible as the feeling of the night air on her cheeks or the angle of the sun or a mad, fleeting desire to learn French or travel to the Southwest. But she gives me books, generously, never holding back, never denying any of my intellectual or emotional desires. She made a rule, you see, a rule she learned from her father when she was small. He said that he might not always be able to give her all the toys or clothes she wanted, but he would never say no to a request for a book. And she's made that the rule for herself and for her children. It's a good rule, and I'm happy that I follow it.

BROOKS
Selected Poems

I lost my original copy when my house burned down. Five weeks after the fire, I found myself aboard a plane to England. On the first night of winter term, he and I met through a mutual acquaintance. We grew close through conversations that would begin in the pub and end in his room. He didn't drink. I'd wake up at his side the next day, both of us fully clothed. One night I told him what happened to my house, my belongings . . . the people who passed. No one here knew what I had seen, and those who had were time zones away. People to whom I had revealed my story tended to drift away afterward. He held me. We grew closer. I was his first.

Upon returning from a solo trip to London, I came back to his room, now littered with my things. On his nightstand was a small gift-wrapped package and a note welcoming me back. I opened the package to find a book that I had been searching for in every bookstore and newsstand I encountered. I once told him how it was hard to find, how he needed to read it if he wanted to know the America that I knew. He gave me a brand-new copy, knowing what had happened to my first.

His last email to me ended with the words, "And now we'll never know." I wish I had left the book with him. I wish I had been a better woman. For all that he gave me in the years since. For all that could never, ever be replaced.

CARD
Ender's Game

"Welcome to the human race. Nobody controls his own life, Ender. The best you can do is choose to fill the roles given you by good people, by people who love you."

I was nineteen when I met him. That first summer together was adventures and night swimming and secrets and reading together in bed. I gave him six or seven of my favorite novels (Salinger and Nabokov, mostly), and in exchange he lent me his copy of *Ender's Game*. This was his favorite book and he had read it countless times.

You can tell almost everything you could need to know about a person by their favorite literature. I found myself relating his behaviors to quotes I found within the text, and so this childhood book of his began to serve as a silent explanation. He fancied himself to be Ender, a tortured boy with the weight of the universe on his shoulders. But he was not a boy; he was a man, and I never saw the humanity in him that I did in Ender.

Two and a half years have passed since I first opened the book, and he and I are strangers now. I have learned that he shares that book with all of the girls he adores, and it was not some testament to our unique bond.

It's a good book, though; I can't really blame him.

DANIELEWSKI
House of Leaves

He was my first boyfriend. I met him the day before my first semester of college. He was ravenously intelligent, a little on the chunky side, and, though I was slow to realize it, an arrogant, pompous asshole. A physics major who, no shit, wanted to find out if the universe was fundamentally computable, he constantly belittled me, a secondary English education major, and enjoyed making me feel stupid and unappreciated. I decided to do the same, and was snide and bitter at every turn. Why I didn't leave him I didn't know, but I do now: you're young, you think you're in love, you think you love someone, you're afraid of being alone, college is scary.

His favorite book was Mark Z. Danielewski's *House of Leaves*. He lent me his copy. I read it. I remember liking it. Now all I can think is that it was like him: void of any real feeling, packed full of useless words, and confusing and infuriating as hell.

Also, though somewhat unrelated, when he first came in my room, he picked up my well-worn, dog-eared, heavily annotated paperback copy of *Ulysses,* which I'd had since high school and loved: my favorite book. He flipped to the last page (to be romantic) and read Molly's final "Yes" . . . and RIPPED IT OUT. Accidentally, of course, but, looking back, I don't see how I couldn't have known it to be an ill omen.

CROWLEY
Little, Big

I met my current girlfriend roughly three years ago. I had a crush on her and she was, of course, dating someone else. After a time I resigned myself to the idea that it wasn't going to happen and we sort of forgot about each other. But later on we were drawn together again, seemingly out of nowhere. At first we defined it as lust, combined with a healthy, adult kind of respect. Whatever it was, it felt kind of inexplicable, as if we really had no control over it.

Early on in our relationship I read John Crowley's classic *Little, Big,* a family saga that begins around the turn of the century and ends sometime in the indefinable future. The Drinkwater family, residing in a rather magical house in upstate New York, could be about as eccentric as any other family in literature, but for one exception: they believe in, and have irrevocable ties to, a secret commonwealth of fairies. The fairies are largely unseen throughout the book, but their presence is felt in numerous ways. They are the orchestrators not only of the fate of the Drinkwater family, but perhaps of fate itself. Struggling with various levels of belief and unbelief, these people are all players in a mysterious design called the Tale.

After I finished it, my girlfriend picked up a copy herself and loved it as much as I did. We were attached to one relationship in the novel particularly, which was that of Smoky Barnable and Alice Drinkwater, whose marriage, though prophesied, is very realistic at the core. Something in us related to, or perhaps craved, the modesty of their love, the quiet dedication to each other that rarely wavers through the years. Also tied up in this is the Tale, which continually taps on their shoulders for the rest of their lives, assuring them in small but inescapable ways that what they're doing is all part of a greater plan.

Little, Big taught us that love is not exactly something flashy, but a solitary thing. It also needs to be worked at in order to thrive. Even if, as we believe to some extent, we have no control over it whatsoever, and that it might just be part of the Tale.

COHEN
Let Us Compare Mythologies

It was a gift for my twenty-ninth birthday. We'd just slept together, and as I lit a cigarette, he rolled over and handed it to me from his backpack. When I saw it I squealed, sat up in bed, and clapped. He was proud of himself, I could tell, pushing back his shoulders and grinning ear to ear.

He was a decade older than I was and constantly worried I'd leave him. He was consumed with insecurity, convinced I might wake up one morning and decide he was too old and that I was bored with him. He never seemed to feel safe enough to be candid about his feelings, and so he inundated me with other people's poetry instead. He was always passing me books wrapped in kraft paper and loose, unlabeled mix CDs in place of his actual feelings, expecting me to mine them for meaning. It was all unwarranted, of course. I loved him ferociously; I was already his. He just didn't seem to have the capacity to believe it, no matter what I said or did.

Afterward we read some of the poems out loud to each other in bed, passing the book back and forth. He isolated one particular excerpt as his favorite, from "The Fly," and read it several times.

We spent the whole beautiful morning together in bed with the windows open, talking, reading, fooling around. It was a perfect day, like something I might have dreamed up and written myself. Later, when he was leaving, I asked him if he would write his name and the date on the inside cover for me.

"Why?" he said, scrunching up his face.

"I don't know . . . it was such a beautiful day, it'd help me remember."

"That's ridiculous," he spat, shaking his head. "What difference would it make?"

"What harm would it do?" I countered.

"No," he said with finality, slipping his foot into his shoe, "that's stupid."

He was always doing that, executing these grand, perfect gestures of affection and then resenting me afterward, as though I'd made him weak by inspiring them. No matter how high he managed to lift me up, he'd inevitably grab for the imaginary upper hand by tearing me down again. I don't know what he thought—if he imagined that chipping away at my self-esteem would make me reliant on him, or what—but it only slowly eroded the love I had for him until it was gone. I did my best to explain that when I left him a year later, but, as usual, he refused to take my word for it, convinced I'd grown bored with him, just as he'd predicted.

CHESTERTON
The Ball and the Cross

You said later that I squeaked when you passed the book to me across the tabletop that night. That morning, rather. We were wearing the days out until we felt paper-thin.

Your inscription was black and terse, but it was then I knew that you knew me. And ever since, we've been kept in this conundrum of straight lines going round and round. And it is in this intersection that I have been brought home.

FISCHER
Saint Ben

I wanted to throw the book down. As if the tears streaming down my face weren't evidence enough that I was upset. This book—this captivating story of a unique little boy told through the eyes of his best friend—was making me cry. It just seemed so very real, as if I myself were the best friend. I was completely drawn in. I couldn't have walked away from the tale then no matter how hard I tried.

There was a wonderful depth in the relationship between young Ben and his friend. I enjoyed it as only a middle school bookworm could. But my twelve-year-old mind was unprepared to feel that depth firsthand as I became engrossed in the story. Reading *Saint Ben* was a gift and a challenge of sorts—to go beyond the adventure of reading, to allow the heart of the story to truly reach me. Of course, I didn't realize that at the time. I just wanted to be able to go back to my teacher and say I had finished it. After all, Mrs. Murrell didn't just lend her books to everyone. She knew I loved to read, but I don't know if she knew how much I hated to cry.

So finish it I did, then dried my tears and put the book away to return later with my thanks. I've read a great many books since then, but the sweet world of *Saint Ben* never quite left my mind. Thanks to Mrs. M's offer, I began to recognize the realness of unreal characters and friendships mean the world to me—even in a fictional world. I still hate to read and cry, but that doesn't stop me from appreciating the beauty of a real story when I see it through tear-filled eyes.

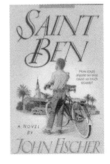

BRASHARES
The Sisterhood of the Traveling Pants

She was a junior and I was a freshman, and we were both on our way overseas. I didn't have anything to read, so she lent me her copy. We found we also shared a love for silly teenage dramas and indie music, and a new friendship was born. This was spring, and life was exciting and new. Our friendship lasted through the next three books and two movies. Through five summers and as many winters. Across two thousand miles and just down the street. But our lives weren't a rosy teenage novel. The distance began to wear on us and emotions began to change. She seemed lonely and clingy to me. I was embarrassed to introduce her to new friends. I felt an obligation to placate her. I wasn't sure if she was still my best friend or a girl who loved me. I can't say what I was to her. I'll never know. There's no longer a sisterhood. No longer any traveling. No longer any love.

DURAS
The Lover

She gave me her copy just before moving in, telling me how it haunted her. She was studying abroad for the year, more exotic and energetic than anyone I knew. During the day she studied drama and in the evening we'd read aloud, quietly. She let me see things through her eyes, and we thought we were in love. I was too young to understand nuance, too dim to see how little she got back from me. I was away traveling when she started an affair, bringing someone else back into my bed. In my rage I burned this book in my kitchen sink, leaving a scar in the countertop. Years later, and she lives in my country, while I live in hers.

SEDARIS
Holidays on Ice

I met S the last semester of my undergraduate degree in Chicago. We shared a class and she was the type of student who read all the extra materials, pulled arguments effortlessly out of the readings, and rolled her eyes unabashedly when she thought someone asked a stupid question. I was in awe of her and therefore avoided contact in fear of receiving a look of disgust. She approached me, however, a few days after she had hit a bicyclist with her car. Apparently my biking to class made me one of the few people she knew who rode regularly and she felt the need to confide in someone familiar with the bicycling community.

I oftentimes think back as to what an awkward first conversation it was to begin one of the most important friendships in my life. Especially since I am in no way, shape, or form an experienced biker.

When I moved to Boston that summer with my boyfriend, I remember thinking our friendship was severely truncated and was pleasantly surprised when she began texting. Our texts turned into emails, letters, bits and bobs, and hours upon hours of phone conversations. My relationship fell apart and, since I was still living in our shared apartment, my long talks on the phone with S would often be the only respite I got from a truly miserable situation.

My ex went to visit his family for Christmas and left me in the apartment alone. I was saving money for a move to San Francisco instead of visiting my own family. I had spent holidays away before, but midway through the day I suddenly felt the need for tradition and went to grab *Holidays on Ice* by David Sedaris. And when it wasn't there, I grabbed the phone with the intentions of distracting myself, but instead broke down and sobbed heavily to S.

The next day she FedExed me her personal copy of the book, inscribed to me.

This copy has accompanied me on numerous Christmases in various cities for years since.

FLEMING
News from Tartary

Since we were both upstaters and about the only sane people in a sitcom-worthy workplace, my coworker and I quickly became friends, despite the generational and class differences between us (he taught at the public school as an act of social justice while I took my tutoring gig out of financial desperation).

Anyway, it was the first semester of my senior year. The night before I had been at Lincoln Center to watch a 1960s Soviet adventure film set in Kazakhstan, and in the morning all I could talk about was how much I wanted to go to central Asia and see the steppes, the mountains, the shrinking Aral Sea. The next day my coworker came in as I was leaving and passed me a book that my chattering had reminded him of. I didn't have a chance to look at it because I had to rush off to a meeting with my undergraduate advisor.

It turned out that this was the absolute last day for me to submit the paperwork for my thesis, and if I couldn't tell my advisor, right then and there, what I was going to write about, I wouldn't be able to graduate with honors. I think I played it pretty cool, considering I had no idea what to say:

"Oh yeah, I've been meaning to talk to you about that. I have one of the primary texts right here." I fished the unknown book out of my bag and held it up to her at such an angle that she couldn't see me frantically scanning the description on the back cover. "The thesis is going to be about . . . British travel writers. In China. During the 1930s." She approved, and I started research that night.

And so I owe quite a lot to my coworker for his prescient reading of my literary taste, especially since the thesis was a bit of a hit and got me into a prestigious, fully funded postgraduate program in Hong Kong, where I continue to study travel writing on central Asia. Thanks, J!

RUSSELL
Moon Rabbit

The book reminded me of us, and that's why I cried. Sitting at my desk behind the employees-only door of the local library where I processed new books, tears seized my whole chest.

I liked to read the new children's books—their tiny spines, sweet pictures, tender stories. They always made me smile, but this one made me cry. It was the story of a little white rabbit who lived alone in the city and longed for a friend. One day, while on a walk through the city, she heard beautiful music and wandered into the country to find its source. The source was a brown rabbit playing his guitar. They talked through the night and he played his music for her to dance to in the moonlight, and she didn't feel lonely anymore.

Like the brown rabbit, M was my best friend. He was my source of music. I talked with him through the night, and without him I felt lonely. He was a receptacle for my secrets, the reader of my silences, a raft I'd set sail in knowing I'd never return.

That wasn't why I cried. I cried because, when the sun came up, the little white rabbit saw the city—her home—in the distance, and missed it. She knew she had to leave her new friend and go home. I cried because I knew, when college ended in a year, M and I would go to our own cities and countries away from each other. Our time was short. We wouldn't be able to talk through every night forever. I bought the book and kept it on my dresser all year.

A few nights before graduation, I wrapped the book and gave it to him as a final present. Crying, I smeared mascara against his nice shirt as he hugged me. I hope one day we get to read the sequel, where brown rabbit comes to the city to visit his friend.

BUKOWSKI
O Capitão Saiu para o Almoço e os Marinheiros Tomaram Conta do Navio

I introduced Bukowski to him, first the poems, and I mentioned that I didn't have a book to lend him 'cause all the books that I've read from Bukowski were the books that I gave my ex-boyfriend. We would spend hours in bookshops and cafés talking about books and music and life, and most of all of how miserable our lives were at that moment, since we both had just left relationships. By then I knew he wanted to be with me, but I couldn't stop thinking about my ex and I thought it wouldn't be fair. But we would still see each other a lot.

Then one day he gave this book to me. It is my favorite Bukowski, and he did a thing that I always do, he read it before giving it to me. Later on he gave me a book of Bukowski poems, and I took him to see a play based on *Ham on Rye*. It was the first play he saw.

This first book that he gave me is made of extracts from Bukowski's journals a few years before his death, and it talks a lot about death, life, and old age.

My friend died in a car accident this year, at the age of twenty-five.

I can only think of how this book made us closer, and I regret that I never had the guts to be with him while he was still alive. And it's funny that since he's gone I can find so much comfort in the books he gave me, and in the words and poems of the dirty old men about death and lost ones.

DE SAINT-EXUPÉRY
Le Petit Prince

The first time we met we kissed in a dodgy nightclub under strobe lights whilst loud music played and then went our separate ways.

We met a few weeks, or months later, in another bar where I had no recollection of him or our kiss. We went on a date to a local park and kissed some more on a bench whilst people walked their dogs and children passed us. I was a shy eighteen-year-old, intimidated by his intense gaze and overwhelmed by his confidence. I refused to see him again.

We reacquainted ourselves whilst he was working in a local homewares shop, where I would walk past and blush when I saw him. He told me about his new girlfriend, and I felt relieved that his intensity was turned away from me. And then we became close friends. He'd come over to my parents' house and drink tea and we'd listen to music together. We kissed once, pressed together on my single bed, our hands all over each other. His girlfriend was correct in being suspicious of us.

He gave me this book for Christmas 2003 with the inscription, "Thanks for being excellent to talk to. You're a great friend, X," and told me it was one of his favourites. I thought, still think, it is a beautiful story, too.

He broke up with his girlfriend and we flirted with the idea of finally getting together. I said, "Can you imagine us having sex?" And burst out laughing.

He just got married, and whilst he was standing at the altar, for a brief moment, I felt sad that I wouldn't be the main focus of his blue-eyed gaze ever again.

BRAINARD
Joe Brainard: I Remember

My boyfriend and I first had that moment of recognition—that we *got* each other—when I sang "Father of Mine" by Everclear at karaoke. We laughed but then said, "I actually think that's a pretty good CD," and that unironic love of Art Alexakis bound us forever.

Later that same night we were hanging out in my kitchen and he saw *The Collected Poems of Frank O'Hara* on my floor. I hadn't met anyone who loved Frank O'Hara as much as I did, and I was in love. He drew a picture of a cow on a notepad and then said, "You should read *I Remember* by Joe Brainard, too. I think you'd really like him." The notepad got tossed aside and I didn't think much about it.

For our first Valentine's Day, he and I built a fort in his living room. We made a big dinner and dessert and we made some funny collages and watched movies in our fort. And that night, he gave me *I Remember*.

I've used it for writing prompts for myself, I've picked it up when I can't sleep and kind of leafed through the pages. He used it in a lesson for a fifth-grade class in which he was teaching a poetry unit as a visiting student teacher. We're still together and we still make forts, but I remember our first Valentine's Day, for sure. I remember a lot.

FAULKS
Birdsong

I was a second-year university student; he was a lawyer, three or four years older than I was. Handsome, charming, blue-eyed, and definitely a grown-up.

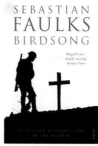

He gave me gifts, wrote me love letters, took me out to dinner, pretty much knocked my socks off. One day he gave me a book: *Birdsong* by Sebastian Faulks.

I took it home and was a chapter or so into it when I came across the first little note, penciled along a line. There were probably about twenty of these notes throughout the book; sweet, loving, sexy notes meant just for me. He somehow did it in a way that wasn't at all cheesy or obvious. And it was impossible to find these notes if I flicked ahead in the book, I had to just stumble across them as I read, like another plotline to an already emotionally intense novel.

A year or so later he broke up with me on a park bench on his morning tea break. I was devastated and cried for an hour in a public toilet nearby. I never forgave him for dropping me in such a cold, cruel manner.

I will, however, always remember that book. I will remember that feeling of being cherished and loved. Of the giddy excitement each note provoked. Of his careful, penciled handwriting fitting snugly into a line on a page.

I don't have the book anymore; I have no idea where it went, but I like to think of other people reading it and wondering about us.

DERRIDA
Limited Inc

Let's be honest: she was clearly humouring me. She was the intelligent one in the relationship. I was the passionate one. She was criticism; I was fantasy. She read Barthes, while I read Tolkien. Her gifting me Derrida's *Limited Inc* was ironic, either that or cruel. A book about language and deconstructionism. If only I had read the book, then maybe I would have seen the warning signs of the end of our relationship. The book sits on my shelf as a reminder: the power of language, communication. Our plans to go to the same postgrad institution didn't work out. She's currently working on her PhD in seventeenth-century early modern drama. I run a hotel. I have no doubt that she's still reading books on linguistics and queer theory; I still read fantasy novels.

GRIMWOOD
Replay

I was floored when this guy I've known for almost three years told me he had this huge crush on me. It never occurred to me before. I just never thought of him that way, and honestly, I really liked him, too. The second time we hung out after that, we discussed time travel. The third time we hung out he brought me this book. His favorite. I am on and off with books: I won't read one for a year, then I'll chew through twelve like nothin'. I flew through this in about two weeks while he and I had this jarring, earth-shattering, incredible love affair. I loved the book and really wanted to talk about it when I finished, but his friend was there at the time, so I couldn't. I gave him MY favorite book and he said he'd make time to read it, even though he's been crazy busy lately. I. Am. In. LOVE!

Then I never saw him again . . . guess he got too busy.

HALL
The Hidden Dimension

July 4, 2011. Gardiner, Maine. Our mutual friends threw a party for the national holiday. He was talking to a friend of mine about the cold. My ears perked up and I chimed in. Not only did we share the love of the chilly weather but also architecture and Chicago. I found a chair, he found one across from me, and we found ourselves in a conversation. The next minutes were filled with questions and coincidences fueled by his passion, photography, TED talks, and art. At the end of the night, he subtly asked me for my phone number.

Two days later he called to chat. I was in the midst of heading to dinner so I said I'd call back. Later that night I did as I promised and we talked about books like *The Fountainhead* and of a recent *New York Times* article on architecture we'd both read. I asked for a book recommendation similar to Ayn Rand's work; and he didn't know of any but mentioned *The Hidden Dimension*. We made plans for the following week.

The platonic hanging out lasted until the beginning of August, when he moved into a new apartment, splitting with his ex-girlfriend. He threw a housewarming party, where he sat next to me while I was conversing with his sister about art, and pulled out the book he had mentioned last time we'd talked. He said I could borrow it, and if I finished that, I may borrow another book in the same series, which he was just finishing up, not for the first time. That night, in an ever so subtle way again, he mentioned how great the Bowdoin College Museum of Art was.

The date went great and we went on to have many others. The book continued to make several appearances in our relationship, from mentions of it on a date in a coffeehouse in Brunswick, to casually citing what Hall had written about anachronistic time. Despite numerous attempts, I never quite got past page forty. The summer was filled with hour-long drives, movie marathons, TV trivia, sarcastic exchanges, midnight walks, late-night gelato runs, moments fueled with caffeine, and never-slumbers.

At the end of October it was time for me to move back to New York City, and he was still in Portland, Maine. I proposed a long-distance relationship, and he accepted. Our schedules were filled with studying, grad school applications, and social obligations. However, whenever we called each other, the moments were filled with glee and laughter, at least on my part.

Three months later I found myself back in Portland, Maine. This time, I arrived with a hope that the romantic sentiments I shared with him would come rushing back the minute I saw him. The stay was filled with moments like the summer but coupled with times of seriousness, the intertwining of his hand and mine, and copious moments of insecurity, more mine than his. This was because, for the first time, I was faced with liking somebody but had no experience in how to deal with it. Questions filled my head, and I did what I always do in moments of panic—I pushed him away. I intentionally hurt him when I did not have the courage to tell and show him how I truly felt: how there were times I wanted to slip his hand into mine when we crossed the street, how his smile was something I always wanted to chase, and how his laughter felt like home. I wanted to hug him so hard when he came from work, like the world was about to end, or to end the night waltzing in the middle of the street. Ultimately, I wanted to tell him how he'd enriched my life and more. Unfortunately, there's a point where the fear and pushing somebody away becomes a permanent state. Things did not work out, and despite his attempts at affection, it became clear how hard those steps to hug him, kiss him, and hold him became.

I still have the novel. Since we've moved from being lovers to being friends, I feel compelled to pick up *The Hidden Dimension* again in hopes of finding the missing pieces of what was so alluring, not just about the book but also about this boy and me.

BULGAKOV
The Master and Margarita

We hadn't met yet but knew we shared a love of literature. His interests trending to the Victorian, I sheepishly admitted to struggling through D. H. Lawrence's *The Rainbow* and requested a pep talk to keep me progressing. He assuaged the guilt caused by both (a) backhandedly scorning a classic, and (b) considering committing the ultimate reading sin, i.e., not finishing a book, by saying that he wasn't a Lawrence fan either, accusations of heresy be damned! When we did meet he brought me one of his copies of *The Master and Margarita* as a suggested replacement. I thought it was so sweet that I almost didn't divulge that I had read it already. But I had and had loved it, so I told him so and gratefully took it to read again. His thoughtful attempt to lift my literary spirits hooked me, and he's done nothing but lift my spirits in general ever since.

ZUSAK
The Book Thief

She found the book at the airport kiosk in Warsaw, on her way back from at trip to Poland she took one November with her husband. I knew them both but at that stage was friends only with her. Friends. Something like that, but closer. Or not. We had known each other a long time, and had shared many a perception, in person and in voice, as we negotiated time together across the bumpy miles. It was often hard to tell what we meant to each other, so alike yet so unlike. But in any case, we both loved books and we loved reading.

She told me about it over the phone when she got back to the States, excited. "I chose it over a copy of *Lamb* and you know that's such a funny and great book. This one's called *The Book Thief*. I picked it up and read it and loved it immediately and reread it on the ten-hour flight back. It's about the war. Nazi Germany. And the book is told by Death. I love it. I *love* it." When she said "I love it" about a book, you could hear her smacking her lips over the phone.

"In fact," she said from her home in the U.S., during one of our cozy telephone chats, "you know those ex-libris stickers you gave me once? I used the very first one, for the first time, for this book."

If she loved a book, chances were I would, too. I would send her books I thought she would like and she would read them ahead of me and opine. I never had the time to read them all but trusted her judgment because I thought, in so many ways, we were as alike as we were unlike. Whatever our disagreements, we could always settle on a book. I sent many books her way and when she had read them, I felt as if I had, too, so I called her my pre-reader. I felt I could reach for it later, with confidence that I might enjoy it or find something new in it because she had liked it. And now here was a book she loved. *Loved.* And vouched for.

"Should I read you the beginning?"

"Of course," I said.

She read, and I was in the book with her.

Death launching an explanation. Death as coy narrator. Death as trickster and witness to human frailty and courage and suffering in Nazi Germany. And the young, orphaned book thief, struggling to understand. I was as enthralled as she. I wanted to read it. But not alone. Not by myself. I wanted to read it through the love she had for the story.

So I suggested she read it to me over the phone since she enjoyed it so much. So much so, she agreed to read over five-hundred and fifty pages out loud over distance and time. She had fallen in love with a wonderful book. And I loved her for loving it.

I never owned the book, but I owned her wonder at it and felt gifted by the time she spent on the phone conveying its complexity. It was a hard book to follow without seeing, remotely, because of the asides, and whimsical, pointed pictures that punctuated it, which she summarized for me. It was a book that exacted attention, as Death danced around the story of the girl, Liesel, and the prose danced around the reader. The entire experience felt like a journey often interrupted but always, always a kind of detour through rapture. What was five-hundred-plus pages when you had all the time in the world with a person you loved to hear read a favorite book to you?

Three years later I traveled to see her at her place, her husband away. We had a devastating falling out. Our friendship was rubble. Even if it was maybe more than strictly friendship. Not all the fiction in the world could put us together again if we had ever been together. Or I had just been telling myself a story, in trust and in love with my pre-reader.

We spoke still, even after she banished me from her presence and from her past. We tried reading together as we had before, and I still sent her books from Canada, as if books could span the loss of trust. "I don't want to read *The Book Thief* to you," the phone said to me in her voice. Page three-hundred and twenty of five-hundred and fifty: that book was over. For me. The gift of this book, retracted forever.

I cannot look at it when I see it on any shelf or reading list. I swivel my head away and walk right by. I will never know how it turned out and what else Death had to say on those pages. I have forfeited my right to this book just as I have lost my pre-reader. And my mind has closed on many memories I once imagined belonged to the both of us, leaving me yet another fool in love with a long-distance story.

ELIOT
Middlemarch

Back in 2004, I got an email from a college friend on Valentine's Day. I'd been trying to get him to read *Middlemarch,* which we'd been assigned in a class we took a few years before (we both skipped it then—bad students!—but I finally tackled it after a long trip spent on planes, trains, and automobiles). Anyhow, in the email he said that he'd read the book, too, and included a favorite quote. I was surprised, as it was the only passage I'd taken the time to write in my journal several months before. I even talked about it with my mom, telling her, "I think this guy might be my soul mate."

Well, I started dating someone else, and then he started dating someone else, and then we were both single and pretty horrible at talking about feelings. But eventually we got married! And my sweet husband gave me a first printing of the full novel (which was originally published in eight parts). Opening it prompted quite the ugly cry. Thank goodness some stories have happy endings.

TOLKIEN
The Silmarillion

When my dad gave me *The Silmarillion* I was amazed. I had already read *The Hobbit* and all of the Lord of the Rings series. I had no idea that there was another book relating to the world of Middle-earth. I read about half of it and discovered that it was the bible of Middle-earth. It told of the beginning and of the end of the story—the end being the end of *The Return of the King*. It was hard to read, though—it was like trying to read Darwin's *On the Origin of the Species*. It was a jumble of names you were supposed to remember. You frequently find yourself lost, looking for the introduction for a character. It explained everything, though; it was just hard to understand. I think everything is like that. It was a fairly old copy; I think it was the one my dad read as a boy. It occupied me for a month or so. It gave me things to think about, as it had my father. That is the gift all books give.

DE SAINT-EXUPÉRY; BATAILLE AND A MYSTERY MAN
Le Petit Prince; Histoire d' l'oeil/Madame Edwarda/Le Mort

My boy-love sent me a copy of Antoine de Saint-Exupéry's *Le Petit Prince,* fragranced with his aftershave and packaged in a gift box of dried wildflowers.

A more, um, mature boyfriend gave me stacks of books throughout our three years together; Georges Bataille's *Histoire de l'oeil* seems most characteristic.

I briefly dated a much older biographer who gave me a copy of one of his own books. If I show the cover, you'll know the man.

Currently I'm seeing someone who hasn't offered me any books. I'm hoping this is a sign that we might actually write our own story together.

YOUNG
Rough Trade

The one he gave me at the very end was the worst. It wasn't the end of the romance, that was long past, but at a time that felt like a gate between the present and the past in our relationship, from a time when we were still involved as good friends to the time when we began to say that we used to be very close. And this book just slapped another metaphorical coat of lacquer on the past-ness of it all, reinforced the notion I'd finally come to understand: we never quite got each other.

We met when we were both extricating ourselves from long-term relationships. Mine was a marriage, half my life long, his was four years with someone he'd once hoped to marry. We delighted in finally, unexpectedly finding each other so compatible. We lived in distant cities, and wrote endless, impassioned emails full of dreams and hopes and deep discussions about love and art and possibility. We chatted nightly on IM, and even risked phone calls when we could do so without rocking our respective sinking ships.

We spent money neither could really afford in order to travel to see each other. And it ended, eventually, ostensibly because the distance of nine hundred miles could never be breached. It wasn't possible for us to be together. But we remained friends, and by chance I did move to his city, but nothing changed. Our friendship was still marked with the same energy and hope—we just figured differently in our dreams for the kind of life we'd have, separately, but still together in some ways.

So, for my birthday, nearly two years later, he gave me a book about a record label on which a band we both loved used to record. But here's the thing: I have no interest in the minutiae of exactly which producer put which songs together or in collecting the six-teen alternate recordings of a beloved song. I don't. He does. He bought the book, and presented it to me on the street right outside the bookshop. And this revealed the brutal truth and the answer to the nagging question of why we hadn't gotten back together. In all our letters, our hundreds of thousands of words exchanged, on screen and in person, we'd explored ourselves more than each other. We were mirrors for each other. Not windows. What we loved in the other was what we most loved in ourselves. The woman to whom he gave the book exists only in his mind. She is not me.

STRUNGE
Samlede Strunge

I got this book for my eighteenth birthday. To celebrate, I invited a few friends over.

The two I considered my best friends gave me two CDs by artists I didn't care about at all. The other three gave me this book.

That's when I realised the friends I'd decided to let go knew me better than the ones I'd decided to keep.

PROSE
My New American Life

He gave me a book. Granted, it is something he got for free at a work-related event, and he swears he'll never get around to reading it himself.

But it's a start.

YOU

Write your own story.

ACKNOWLEDGMENTS

Thanks for this project must go first to the amazing community of readers and writers I've come to know through TheBooks TheyGaveMe.com. What started with just a clever, cool idea has grown into something tremendous. I always knew that I wasn't the only one who connects the dots of her life through the books I have read, but I'm not sure I realized how very many of us there are. Thank you to all who have read, shared, and contributed to the blog.

Next, I must offer my heartfelt love and gratitude to all my family and friends: John and Edward, Patricia and Dennis Adams, and Sarah Hawley chief among them. Also my wonderful, eccentric, beautiful adoptive family of fellow New Yorkers: Carla Barrett, Nick Shuit, Lauren Bowling, Megan Stroup, Sam Howard-Spink, Evan Michelson, Chris Kuty, and everyone at Scopia. You have each been a partner to my success here, and I thank you.

My agents, Adam Schear and Brian DeFiore, and editors Leslie Meredith and Donna Loffredo deserve huge thanks and big bouquets of roses for believing in this project and coaxing me through the process. Rachel Fershleiser and everyone at tumblr deserve my utmost gratitude for providing the architecture upon which so many wonderful connections are being built.

Most important, I wish to thank those whose stories are in this book—both those listed here and those who have chosen to remain anonymous:

A. C. Hurd

Aaron Thomas

Adam Salazar

Alana Westwood

Alex Greenberg

Alexandra Faulkner

Alicia J. Arnold

Alix Iovieno

Andrew Broussard

Angela Tung

Anonymous

April Kinkade

Beth Neiman

Brittany Owens

C. G. Farolan

C. K. McKay

Cait Poynor Lamberton

Caitlin M. Lord

Camille C. Garcia

Carla Barrett

Caroline Sarah

Casey Coleman

Catherine Corman

ccn

Christi Griffis

Christopher Walker

Clint Slaugenhaupt

Cyndy Aleo

Daniel Roberts

David Good

Douglas Riggs

Edward Donnelly

Elizabeth Taddonio

Ellen Ratchye

Emilia Mary

Emily Perper

Emma Aylor

Fan Yue (Claudia) Mang

francesco vitelli

G. S.

Gabriel Sousa

Gunjana Dey

Hannah Park

Hännah Schellhase

Harini Venkatesan

Heather Aubrey Meadows

Henric Fröberg

J Gaines

Jacquelynn Bourdon

Jaime

Jay Pinho

Jen Lazar

Jen Leija

Jennifer A. Chick

Jesse Sheidlower

Jessica Lechtenberg

John Galiatsos

Jon Johnson

Joy Ling

Kara Gaughen

Kara Stephanie Gordon
Kathleen O'Neill
Katie Day
Katy Anne Rosell
Kellie Harris
Kendall Kulper
Kimberly Binkley
Kristina Ringstrom
Laura R. Olcheski
Lauren Bowling
Lauren C. DiCintio
Lauren A. Sepanski
Leah D.
Lindsay Rainingbird
Lindsey C. Turner
Liz Shannon Miller
Liz Sofman
Lorenzo Alunni
Mary Alice Martin
Megan M. Richardson
Megan Stroup

Melissa Reburiano
Miladine Etienne
Molly Fessler
Nicholas Freilich
Niki Aguirre
Nikki Smith
Pariesa Young
Petra Magno
Preeti K.
Rachelle Rowe
Rebecca C. Hansen
Ruchira Ray
Rushda Rafeek
Sarah Williams
Sharline Bareng
Stephen Parolini
Tiffany Scolnic
Toni Lupro
Yan Khalis
Yevgeniy Levitskiy
Zoelle Cooksey

ABOUT THE AUTHOR

After a decade and a half spent in Chicago, where she worked as a freelance writer and served as a founding contributing editor of *Digital Scrapbooking* magazine, Jen Adams moved to New York to be closer to the Strand. She is at work on a variety of projects, including a zombie novel for middle-grade readers. She blogs at Jen-Adams.com. She lives in Astoria, New York, and is the mother of two boys.